EVERYDAY SAINT

REJECTING SIN, CHOOSING LOVE

JIM HAMPTON

D0026903

{ UNDERCURRENT SERIES }

Barefoot Ministries®
Kansas City, Missouri

ISBN 978-0-8341-5018-8

Printed in the United States of America

Editor: Bo Cassell
Assistant Editors: Stephanie McNelly & Stephanie Harris
Cover Design: Lindsey Rohner
Interior Design: Sharon Page

Library of Congress Cataloging-in-Publication Data

Hampton, Jim, 1966-
     Everyday saint : rejecting sin, choosing love / Jim Hampton.
        p. cm.
     ISBN 978-0-8341-5018-8
  1. Christian teenagers—Religious life. 2. Holiness—Christianity. I. Title.
     BV4531.3.H36 2007
     248.8'3—dc22

                                                                          2007011962

10 9 8 7 6 5 4 3 2 1

"'Who are you?' Leilani Klonk asks the ten-year-old boy.

"He answers, 'I am **being** Curtis Hammond.'

"Though unaware, Leilani has just begun a relationship with an extra-terrestrial that is in the process of morphing into a new creature."

Dean Koontz, *One Door Away from Heaven*[1]

This book is dedicated to the millions of teenagers who are **being** holy people, morphing into the person that God created them to be. May you find it helpful in your passionate pursuit of holiness.

CONTENTS

ACKNOWLEDGMENTS   7

INTRODUCTION   9

    Chapter 1: What Holiness Is . . . and Isn't   15

SECTION 1: FREEDOM FROM SIN—HOLINESS AS PURITY   25

    Chapter 2: Undivided Loyalties—Loving God More Than Ourselves   27

    Chapter 3: Breaking the Chains—Experiencing Liberation   38
        from Sin

SECTION 2: FREEDOM FOR GOD—HOLINESS AS LOVE   51

    Chapter 4: The Perfect Love—Responding in Obedience   53

SECTION 3: FREEDOM FOR OTHERS—   71
        HOLINESS AS CHARACTER AND POWER

    Chapter 5: Chasing Lions—Choosing to Love Others for   73
        the Sake of God

    Chapter 6: Lions and Lambs—The Communities that   86
        Shape Our Character

CONCLUSION: EVERYDAY SAINTS—LIVING AS HOLY PEOPLE   97

GLOSSARY OF HOLINESS TERMS   105

SUGGESTED RESOURCES FOR FURTHER STUDY   107

NOTES   109

ACKNOWLEDGMENTS

It's a good sign when one writes a book and learns much in the process. While I have degrees in religious studies, I found the process of reading through the preparatory material for this book to be very helpful in that it forced me to move beyond my normal theological words and find ways to express these great concepts in new words that youth and young adults could understand. Toward that end, I'm indebted to two groups of people:

- The professors who both taught me and who are now my colleagues—those at Mount Vernon Nazarene University, Nazarene Theological Seminary, and Asbury Theological Seminary. Your passion in helping me develop my own passion for God and His holiness is incalculable; and
- The thousands of teenagers and college students I've had the opportunity to work with in nearly 20 years of youth ministry. Your insightful questions and unwillingness to accept shallow answers have forced me time and time again to be more thoughtful and complete in my writing and speaking.

INTRODUCTION

Holiness. What comes to mind when you hear this word?

I've talked with thousands of high school and college age students over the last 20 years. Here are just a few of the descriptions I've heard them use to describe holiness:

- "The 'holy people' I've met seem to have no joy. They are people who walk around looking like their best friend just died. Why would I want to be like that?"—Omar, age 20.
- "It's all about the rules you have to follow—lots and lots and lots of rules!"—Josh, age 14.
- "Holiness? Doesn't that mean you never have any fun?"—Lucy, age 13.
- "It means obeying the 10 commandments, going to church, reading your Bible, doing daily devotions, praying, and being a good influence on others."—Kristen, age 13.
- "What does holiness mean? Truthfully, I have no idea."—Josh, age 14.
- "I think it means you have to be perfect . . . which leaves me out!"—Marissa, age 21.
- "My pastor told me it was all about being perfect, and that once I was sanctified, I'd never have to deal with sin again. To tell you the truth, I just can't buy into that. I mean, have you ever met someone who didn't sin anymore? It seems like an impossible thing to me."—Jordan, age 18.
- "Aren't people who are holy kind of stuck up? They act all 'holier-than-thou' as if they were better than me."—Joaquin, age 16.
- "Is it possible to be holy? I don't know. I don't often feel very holy. More times than I can count I find myself being tempted by things around me, so I know that I must not be holy. I guess it works for others, but I'm just not sure that I can be holy."—Juanita, age 20.

All of these descriptions have one thing in common—they do NOT describe the biblical understanding of what it means to be holy!

And to tell you the truth, I'm discouraged by all the wrong understandings of holiness that are floating about—understandings that, more often than not, cause people to believe that they can never really be holy.

9

In fact, I would suggest to you that these wrong descriptions of holiness are what keep most people from really experiencing and living out God's incredibly life-transforming gift of holiness as described in the Bible.

That's why this book was written. You see, I've devoted most of my life to helping young people discover what it means to truly fall in love with God. Too often, the relationship that students (and many adults as well) have with God is a pale imitation of what could be. They have yet to tap into the potential of what God is offering them. There are many reasons for this, most of which could be boiled down to one—they have not been told nor have they seen what real, biblical holiness looks, smells, and acts like. In other words, they are following a counterfeit version of holiness.

I've been told that people who handle money a lot (bank tellers, cashiers, etc.) do not take classes or spend time learning about counterfeit money. If I were a banker, I would want all of my employees to know everything there was about the different types of counterfeit bills that might be floating around so they could instantly recognize it if someone tried to pass a fake bill. But they don't.

The problem is that there are so many good forgeries around that to study counterfeit bills is both time consuming and inefficient. Instead, these money handlers study real money. They know it incredibly well— they know how it feels, what it looks like, what it tastes like (some actually do taste the paper bills), and even what it smells like. They spend so much time getting to know the real thing—really becoming intimately familiar with it—that when a counterfeit bill slips through, they can detect it immediately. They know that it isn't the real thing.

I want to suggest that you and I need to become just like those bankers. We should know Jesus so incredibly well that we will know immediately when something is not of God. We should have such an intimate, loving, soul-changing relationship with Jesus that anything that is even the least bit different from who God is and what He wants will stand out like a sore thumb. That's how we know that those unattractive and counterfeit views of holiness are wrong. Jesus was not like that.

FOUR WAYS TO KNOW

So how do we know what Jesus was like? In the Wesleyan tradition,[2] they talk about four ways through which we come to know Him—the Holy *Scriptures*, Church *tradition*, the ability to *reason* with our minds, and personal and corporate *experience*. Quadrilateral

10

- **Scripture.** The Bible gives us an up-close-and-personal look at Jesus as recorded by those closest to Him. Scripture is the most important element for helping us know who Jesus is. It speaks to us by showing us the life Jesus lived; we then compare our own lives (our experiences) to His as we seek to imitate Him.
- **Tradition.** The church has held fast to its understanding of who Jesus is as recorded in the historic creeds. These creeds describe Jesus as being one with God, yet willingly coming to earth through a virgin birth, in order that He might eventually die for our sins, and through His resurrection from the dead, offer us new and eternal life. Today, that tradition continues to be written by the church's theologians, Bible scholars, and other pastors and teachers of the faith.
- **Reason.** The more that science uncovers, the more complexity that is revealed, the more evident it is that there had to have been an originator, a creator, of all that is. I have no idea exactly how God did it—I just know that He did. The way we discover these things is by using the remarkable brain that God has chosen to give us. With this brain, we have the ability to critically analyze complex situations and come to solutions. We understand that all truth is from God, regardless of where we may find it—in Scripture, in science, or in the rational, logical thought of our minds. As we seek to better understand who God is and how we are to live, we use the resources God has given us—and one of those is reason.
- **Experience.** You and I each have life experiences that shape us. Because our experiences are so richly varied depending on our life situation, it produces a beautiful mosaic of the ways Jesus is at work in our lives. Our experiences inform our reading of the biblical message, and the biblical message should naturally shape the way we live our lives.

Over the course of this book, we will use all four ways to examine this concept called holiness. We will endeavor together to see what the Bible, tradition, our God-given ability to reason, and our own personal and corporate experiences tell us about who Jesus is. As we learn that, we discover together what holiness is . . . and is not.

FAN OR FRIEND?

Once while waiting for a flight, I was browsing through the airport stores. I eventually wandered into the bookstore, where I saw Antonio

Banderas, the actor. I couldn't pass up the opportunity; I just had to meet him. So I went up to him and said, "I'm a big fan of yours."

He smiled, shook my hand, said "Thank you," and then walked away.

Now, if I was to ever run into Banderas again, what do you think are the chances that he would remember me? One in a million? Less? I would almost guarantee that he would have no clue who I was, nor that we had ever met before. Why? Because we had no relationship. It was a chance encounter, probably never to occur again. If somehow I beat the odds and we ended up face-to-face again, Banderas would have no reason to recall that we had met.

When I consider the subject of holiness, I sometimes wonder, "What would happen if I met Jesus today? Would He recognize me?"

Let's switch places. You're at the airport, browsing in the bookstore, and in walks Jesus. If you approached Him, stuck out your hand and said, "Hi, Jesus. I'm a HUGE fan of Yours; I follow You every day," how would He respond to you? Would He wrap His arms around you in a warm embrace and say, "I know who you are. After all, we talk daily, and you invite Me along everywhere you go." Or would He politely shake your hand, say a word of thanks, and move on, wondering who this stranger was who had interrupted His walk.

You see, we live in a world where people routinely do just enough to get by. Unfortunately, that sometimes creeps into the way we approach the issue of holiness—we only scratch the surface without ever really allowing God to show us what could be. We spend just enough time with Jesus to feel better about ourselves, but not enough time to allow Him the opportunity to really begin to shape our lives to better reflect His life. The reality is this: until Jesus becomes our sole focus in life—the One we seek to follow more than anyone or anything else—we will never experience what it means to be holy as God is holy.

As we study together, my simple prayer is that you will catch a vision for what holiness really is by looking first and foremost to see who Jesus is, and just as importantly, that you will commit yourself wholly to Him—body, mind, soul, and spirit—so that He can truly make you a holy person.

USING THIS BOOK

At the end of each chapter, you will find a series of questions designed to help you think more critically about holiness. These questions fall under three headings:

- **Questions to Ponder**—you will be asked to review and analyze the material read in that chapter.
- **Emotions to Process**—you will be asked to consider how the chapter is impacting you, and the feelings and emotions that you are processing as you allow these concepts to infiltrate your life.
- **Actions to Practice**—these questions are designed to help you apply the principles you learn in this book to everyday life. As such, this section will often ask you to engage in practices which will reinforce the ideas presented in the chapter.

It's easy to read the chapters and just give quick, superficial answers to the questions or even to ignore them altogether. Let me ask you not to do this. Educators have long known that one of the best ways to ensure that learning and growth are taking place is to immediately begin to review and process the information you've received. So please carefully consider the questions, work through them slowly (writing your answers in a journal, if you so desire), and let them seep into you. Perhaps as you work through this book the Spirit of God will reveal himself to you and you will begin to journey into this wonderful life called holiness.

Blessings on you as you seek to become like our Holy God!

CHAPTER 1
WHAT HOLINESS IS
. . . AND ISN'T

"Love takes the Harshness out of Holiness"
—Mildred Bangs Wynkoop, Theology of Love

Holiness is a buzz word in Christian circles these days. And it's not just one group or denomination that is focusing on this topic. Rather, there are numerous groups and denominations who have become infatuated with this crucial doctrine of the Christian faith. Unfortunately, while many of these groups are writing and talking about holiness, they present holiness in a way that is not compatible with traditional Christian teaching. For these groups, holiness is all about God and has nothing to do with us. In fact, they would argue, it is impossible for humans to be holy because holiness is the sole domain of God. But is that true? Can only God be holy?

It is certainly true that holiness comes out of God and is who God is—but it is equally true, according to Scripture, that you and I can also be holy because of God. Otherwise why would God command us, "I am the LORD your God; consecrate yourselves and be holy, because I am holy . . . I am the LORD, who brought you up out of Egypt to be your God; therefore be holy, because I am holy" (Leviticus 11:44-45)?

REDEFINING THE WORD

It may help to define what we mean by the word "holy." In the Introduction, we looked at several honest, but not very accurate, definitions of holiness. As part of my preparation to write this book, I asked several teenagers, youth pastors, and professors how they would define holiness. Here are just a few of the definitions these folks contributed to the discussion:

Holiness is . . .

- "to live like Christ—a life of self-sacrificing love."—Eric, a teenager
- "being baptized by the Holy Spirit, who then lives in our hearts." —Jazmine, a teenager

- "living together with other Christians as we seek to live out what it means to be part of the kingdom of God on earth."—Rudy, a teenager
- "to be set apart for God and His work, to be cleansed of all sin, to be perfect, and to avoid sin from here on out—but the most fundamental meaning is love."—Tom, a professor
- "the reflection of God's own character."—Wes, a pastor
- "loving God with all your heart, soul, mind, and strength and our neighbor as ourselves."—Deirdre, a pastor
- "Holiness is the place where love and justice meet."—Ruth Anne, a professor
- "giving control over every aspect of my life to God and letting Him be in charge. Some people call this 'dying out to self'."—Troy, a youth pastor

If nothing else, these definitions of holiness should serve to help us understand something very important—namely, that there are lots of different ways to talk about holiness! Each of the definitions above emphasizes an important aspect of what it means to be holy. The problem, from my perspective, is that far too often we focus on these various individual parts of holiness rather than seeking to explore the *whole* of holiness.

NARROWING IT DOWN

When I was growing up, I was often confused by all the different and segmented ways that people talked about holiness. It was not uncommon to hear my pastor talk about holiness using one set of words (such as "purity" and "sanctification") while my parents used another set of words (e.g. "love" and "Christlikeness") and to hear yet another set of words used at camp or when we had a revival (words like "eradication" and "dying out to self"). The problem, far too often, was that these women and men seemed to be offering me ideas that were similar at best and contradictory at worst in the way they described holiness to me. It seemed to me that everyone was talking about a different understanding of holiness. As a result, holiness seemed to me to be some unattainable goal. After all, if those who knew it best couldn't agree on what it was, how could I possibly live it out?

Fortunately, I eventually came to understand that there weren't really competing or even different definitions of holiness. Rather they were simply different slices of the same pie. In other words, each person who talked about holiness talked about a *small segment* of it, rather than the *whole*. That's why it always seemed as if they were talking past each other.

It would be good to look at holiness as one whole idea. To do this means that we begin to look beyond our limited view of holiness and capture the bigger picture of what holiness is, what it does, and what it looks like in our lives.

In this book I will do my best to dispense with using ten-dollar words about which everyone has a differing opinion. Instead, we will focus on who Jesus is and what He desires for our lives, since Jesus is the center of what it means to be holy. Therefore, the working definition of holiness for this book is as follows: **Holiness is Christlikeness**. A plain and simple definition, and yet one which we will spend the rest of this book unpacking.[3]

IN THE BEGINNING

As we begin our study of what it means to be holy, perhaps we should start at the very beginning, Genesis 1—3. Go ahead and grab your Bible as we look at this together.

God had graciously given to Adam and Eve that which He had not given to any other creature that He created—the gift of being made in His image. Think about that for a moment. God, the awesome creator of the universe who is the epitome of what it means to be holy, created us in His image (Genesis 1:27). From the very beginning of time, God intended that we would be like Him.

Since God intends that we be like Him, He created us so that our hearts would naturally turn to Him. God's plan was that our worlds would revolve around Him and that everything we chose to do would be because of who He is and what He wants us to be. For Adam and Eve, this meant that they would care for the garden and rule over the other created beings as God's representatives (Genesis 1:28; 2:15-17).

But, as so often happens in great stories, there was a dramatic plot twist—free-will. When God created Adam and Eve, He instilled in them the ability to say "No," to choose their own way rather than God's way. This was necessary to ensure that the love Adam and Eve had for God (and that we have for God) was genuine and not forced. God wanted to make sure that we were following Him because we wanted to, not because we had to. Otherwise, it wouldn't really be love.

Of course, granting free-will meant that when Adam and Eve were presented with an alternative to God's plan, they had the ability to choose to do things their way rather than God's way. Enter the tree from which they were told not to eat. There was no reason given, just a stern warning accompanied by an even sterner punishment if they violated the command.

As temptations often do, the serpent comes into the story almost without our realizing it and immediately begins to cast doubt upon what God has said. Eve and the serpent begin to debate and interpret God's words. A discussion takes place about which fruit God was talking about, and whether they would really die if they ate it.

Go back and read Genesis 3:1-5, noticing Eve's language. Up until this point, the young woman has always been in conversation with God. However, now, for the first time in her young life, the woman is not talking to God but rather *about* God! No longer is God a person with whom she relates, the One with whom she has daily walks in the Garden. Instead, He is now an object she talks about indirectly. The very prohibition which once seemed a given is now scrutinized by Eve, as though it were not a given, but an option. God's rule is no longer a boundary to be observed but an obstacle to be avoided. She stands at the tree, gazes longingly at the fruit, and then reaches up, plucks some, and eats it. She then seeks out her husband, and he also eats from the tree.

As they eat, their eyes are opened. But instead of the terrific rush of wisdom coursing through their heads, a sense of shame fills them. Where before their nakedness had been something they mutually enjoyed, now it was something of which they were ashamed. No longer are they guiltless in their relation with one another or with God. So they cover themselves, and in the process, lose the intimacy they had once known. "Sin can be described as love gone astray or love that has been misdirected and distorted. It is a perversion of Christian love."[4] This is the reality that Adam and Eve have discovered.

While they are wrestling with this new and terrible dilemma, they hear a sound that they have heard so many times before—God walking in the garden. That sound had always brought joy before, but this time it inexplicably brings feelings of panic and fright. They must hide! Quickly moving in among the bushes and shrubs, the man and the woman attempt to do what so many people since them have tried in vain—to hide from a seeking God. They realize that they are naked and defenseless. God now looks threatening. The question "Where are you?" (Genesis 3:9) is not heard as an inquiry but as an accusation. So they hide.

This rebellion of our first parents is alive and well today. Because of Adam and Eve's decision to disobey God, we all have within us a predisposition to want things our way, rather than God's way. This inclination toward self-sufficiency, more than any other thing, is what keeps us from being able to be holy. Instead, we find ourselves seeking to please ourselves, fulfilling our own wants and wishes rather than pleasing God and desiring what He desires. It's a classic battle of wills—our will versus God's will. And as long as we continue to allow our will to reign supreme, it is impossible for us to be holy people. As long as I claim control of any part of my life, then Adam's sin is still present. In fact, until I am willing to acknowledge God's claims upon my life and then unequivocally give Him all that I have, this sin of rebellion continues within me.

However, there is hope, as Adam and Eve discovered. God, as He does so often, continues to call out to them. The man and the woman soon realize that they will have to answer for their actions. They each admit their guilt but pass the blame for their actions to someone else—the woman, the serpent, even God himself.

God passes His judgment upon the man, woman, and serpent. Just as the man and the woman had perverted their relationship with God and each other, so their sentences make their lives perversions of God's original intention.

As they leave the garden, the man and woman are perplexed. Had not God said, "In the day that you eat of this fruit, you will die?" Why are they still alive? Their punishment seems so small and inconsequential compared to what God has promised. Then they begin to think back over the last several hours. There had been peace and harmony; now there was division and strife. Before, the land had been so easy to plant and cultivate; now there would be hard work. Before, the woman was told to populate the earth; now there would be great pain associated with birth. In the garden, they had enjoyed the presence of the Creator; now they were on their own. As they contemplate this, they step out of the garden for the first time. They look upon a barren landscape so different from what they had enjoyed. Suddenly, the truth hits them with the force of a hurricane. They are dead.

You see, they had been removed from the very presence of God. No longer could they enjoy their evening walks in the garden conversing with God. No longer would they be able to spend time in God's presence, learning what He wanted. No longer were these creatures, made in God's image, reflecting what God desired. Instead, they were now following their own way of life, one which differed significantly from God's plan.

THE PROBLEM WITH BEING INDEPENDENT

I want to suggest that what is wrong in this world, wrong in our relationships with each other and with God, is the direct result of our insistence on denying our absolute dependence on God. Humans have always been restless and dissatisfied with what we have—as long as we are aware of something more, something we do not yet possess. And the ultimate possession would be to own ourselves—to be our own bosses, responsible to no one—to be god. (Notice the difference between being created in His image, being like Him—and replacing Him.)

We must understand that God's prohibition on the tree of the knowledge of good and evil was not meant to deprive the man and the woman of something positive. Instead it was to keep them from experiencing pain, hurt, disappointment, and betrayal. It was meant to keep from humanity what is possibly the greatest burden we have ever taken upon ourselves—that of being separate and independent from God.

Do we understand then what the man and the woman failed to realize until it was much too late? Our refusal to live in the context of a right relationship with God, choosing to follow our way instead of God's, is ultimately what makes us unholy. The man and the woman were created by God to live in proper relation to Him; as long as they did this, there was peace and harmony. They lived in community with God and each other. They were able to live out what it meant to be created in God's image because they had the ultimate example of that image to follow. But when they decided that they knew what was best and rejected God's rule, discord and strife entered their lives. No longer was there a sense of trust and love between God and humans, or even between humans and other humans.

RETURNING TO GOD-RULE

Even though we are the fallen children of Adam and Eve, we are still created in God's image. As such, we are called to establish a proper relationship with God. It is God, and God alone, who knows what is best for us. He is the source of life and the sustainer of life. We have to learn to trust His goodness and be willing to submit to His wisdom and ways. We have to be willing to turn from our self-rule and turn toward God-rule in our lives. It is only when we allow God to guide us in our living that we can establish right relationships with those around us. In short, holiness is about our willingness to allow God to bring all parts of our life under the rule of His kingdom.[5] Augustine, one of our early church fathers, describes the relationship this way: "Without God, we cannot; without us, God will not." Holiness is a willing response to God. We accept God's gracious invitation to repair that primary relationship with Him, and in so doing, we are restored to God's original intent—that we become holy people created in God's image to serve Him and the world around us.

A HOLY PEOPLE

Becoming holy people doesn't happen overnight. It really does take a lifetime of practice. Think of it this way. Remember when you were first learning to ride a bike without training wheels? You didn't just hop on and race down the street. First you had to learn to balance; then you had to have mom or dad hold on to the seat while you wobbled your way along. You may have run over dad's toes a few times as he ran alongside helping you steer straight. You probably fell off a few times, got frustrated, and maybe even thought of giving up because it just wasn't worth the effort. But eventually, several skinned knees, many apologies to your dad, and lots of practice later, you were able to ride down the sidewalk. You had mastered the two-wheel bike!

That's the way it is with this journey called holiness. We begin to be holy people by joining ourselves to Jesus. Our initial steps in following Him become the first steps in a holy life.[6] From that moment forward, we embark on this exciting journey called holiness, where God is already at work to make us holy people . . . if we will let Him.

However, none of us are good or talented or bright enough to do it well right away. It takes practice—a lifetime's worth—to really master what it means to be holy. It often takes some skinned knees when we try to rush the process instead of waiting for God's timing. And it can even mean that in our zeal to follow God we inadvertently run over a few toes, forgetting that others are on the same journey. But all along the way, we are learning what it means to be holy.

THE DISCIPLES' ROAD

Consider the twelve disciples chosen by Jesus. These 12 men had the awesome privilege of spending 3 years with Jesus—eating with Him, traveling with Him, listening to Him, praying with Him, sharing their deepest needs and dreams with Him. He called each one of them to come and follow Him, and when they did, they became different. The more time they spent with Jesus, the more they began to live in a different way. As they tried to emulate Him, they found themselves meeting with people they would have previously avoided—those who were sinners, demon possessed, and shunned by organized religion. They participated in miracles such as the feeding of the 5,000, witnessed people being cured from all sorts of diseases, and saw Lazarus raised from the dead.

What qualified them to do these things? Had they gone to the best Jewish college and majored in religion? Did they attend seminary and study theology? Were they trained by the best scholars and practitioners of ministry in their day? No. The disciples were at best just simple, common men. In fact, most of them were just fishermen—men of ordinary means. What made them different? One thing and one thing only—being with Jesus, the Holy One. When He was with them, and they with Him, they were holy. Jesus is what made them extraordinary.

And yet . . . one of those men, Judas, agreed to betray Jesus to the Roman soldiers for a handful of coins. Another, Peter, who had pledged his very life for Jesus, ended up denying that he even knew Jesus—three times. And Thomas, upon hearing that Jesus had been resurrected from the dead as He promised, refused to believe it without tangible evidence. And the other disciples? When Jesus was crucified they tucked their tails and ran away, hiding behind locked doors for fear that they would be the next ones arrested and killed.

So, were the disciples holy? Yes. Like us, God had already begun this work in their lives. But they recognized, as we must, that holiness does not occur all at once. It is a lifetime pursuit. One of the counterfeit ideas about holiness is that holiness is a static thing to have, something that we possess rather than a life we live. In other words, some people believe that God makes us completely holy at a certain moment and that's the end. We are now completely holy and never again have to worry about sin. However, examples from Scripture seem to indicate that this is not the case. God calls us to a life of holiness from the moment we ask Him to forgive us of our sins and agree to follow Him, but He spends *the rest of our lives* completing that process. It was true for the first disciples, and is true for us.

We begin to be holy people the moment we choose to follow Jesus.

Our initial steps in following Him become the first steps in a holy life. But we are not finished. Just like our bicycle experience, it takes practice before we are at a point where we don't have to worry constantly about falling prey to sinful temptations. And even when we get to the point where we are riding without the training wheels, we still have to be on constant guard for those potholes along the way which can trip us up. Once we begin walking with God, we have to stay "in step with the Spirit." (Galatians 5:25).

What enables us to not only survive the journey, but actually thrive and enjoy it, is the fact that we don't make the journey alone. Jesus, who has been with us from the very beginning, continues to walk beside us, helping us navigate this road called life. It is through His power, love, and guidance that we are enabled to continue to grow in holiness, becoming more and more like Him in our words, actions, and attitudes. We can see what holiness looks like and how holiness behaves by watching Jesus. And the more our focus is on Jesus, the less we will worry about doing things that aren't like Jesus. But the key is spending time with Him. We'll discuss this more in the following chapters.

Questions to Ponder

1. How would you have defined holiness prior to reading this chapter? How would you define it now?
2. Do you really believe that it is possible for humans to be holy? Do you believe that you can be holy? Why or why not?
3. What are some of the counterfeit ideas about holiness that you've heard?

Feelings to Process

1. When we hear the word "holiness," certain images come to mind. What are some of those images which have shaped the way you feel about holiness?
2. When you think of a holy God, how does that make you feel? Terrified? In awe? Confused? Ashamed? Part of the team?
3. How is your story like Adam and Eve's? How is it different?

Actions to Practice

1. Earlier in this chapter, you read this quote from Augustine: "Without God, we cannot; without us, God will not." Consider what your role is in this pursuit of holiness. Write a short prayer to God, let-

ting Him know that you're committed to this process of becoming a holy person.

2. Working through this book by yourself might be confusing. Find a trusted Christian with whom you can discuss the things you read, as you seek to become the person God created you to be.

SECTION 1

FREEDOM FROM SIN
HOLINESS AS PURITY

CHAPTER 2

UNDIVIDED LOYALTIES
LOVING GOD MORE
THAN OURSELVES

*"You formed us for yourself, and our hearts are restless
till they find rest in you."—Augustine,* Confessions

Have you ever been really thirsty? I'm not just talking about wanting a sip; I'm talking about tongue-swelling, cotton-mouth thirsty. I've been there. I was in eighth grade, and we had just lost to a football team that we should have crushed. Our coach was so angry that he ordered us to remain completely silent on the way home . . . or else. Well, one of my wonderful teammates couldn't resist trying to talk to one of the cheerleaders. Our coach overheard them and told us that we would truly suffer the next day. Since our coach was not the type to make lighthearted promises, I was a little worried.

The next day, we dressed for practice and went out to face our coach in the ninety degree weather. He started off by blistering us for our poor showing the day before. Then, when our egos were completely destroyed, he attempted to do the same thing to our bodies. He ordered us to start running laps around the football field. He told us to just start running; he would let us know when our punishment was up. So run we did.

One lap, two laps, three laps. We really started wondering just how mad our coach was. Thirteen laps, fourteen laps, fifteen laps. By this time our mouths were parched and our throats burned. Twenty-two laps, twenty-three laps, twenty-four laps. Finally, six miles after we started, the whistle sounded.

Fortunately, he had some compassion and allowed us to go to the water fountains. Now you would think that a group of people who had just run six miles would be completely devoid of any energy, but the moment he mentioned cool, refreshing water, something inside each of us came alive. We made a mad dash for the water fountains and gulped the water down as fast as we could swallow.

I'll tell you, nothing mattered more to me at that moment than water. It was all I cared about, all I could think of. It ruled my life. Nothing could have gotten me moving again except the prospect of water. Why? Because I realized that if I was to survive, I would need water. It was so basic that nothing else mattered.

Something like that single-minded passion describes the type of relationship you and I are called to have with Jesus Christ.

The reality, however, is that for too many of us, there are a whole host of competing loyalties. When we asked Jesus to forgive our sins and invited Him into our lives, we really meant it. The problem was that we had forgotten about all of the other things in our lives which weren't compatible with who Jesus is. And soon, there developed a battle of sorts, as we wrestled with which loyalties we were going to follow. While most Christians claim they only worship one God, they show in practice that they actually serve several gods because their loyalties are spread out. God really doesn't have their total allegiance.

THE LOYALTY STRUGGLE

The list of potential loyalties which we have is long—far too long to list them all here. But there are some things to which we give our loyalty which seem to be common. Let me mention just a few by sharing some examples. All of the names have been changed so as not to cause embarrassment.

Miranda, who came from a great Christian family, gave her life to Jesus as a little girl. Now at 16, she was a natural leader who had a charismatic personality which naturally attracted others. She seemed to have everything going for her; however, she had one small problem—she was dating Chad, a non-Christian.

It was evident that Miranda had a loyalty problem. What God wanted for Miranda and what Chad wanted for her were very different. Miranda recognized the difference but was torn over how to respond. She knew that God wanted all of her, but she knew that if she gave her entire being to God, more than likely Chad would have to go. Miranda struggled with which person would have her ultimate loyalty—God or Chad.

Manuel came from a poor family—his parents had immigrated to the United States when he was a baby, and they didn't have any marketable skills by which to secure employment. They wanted better for the children, so they worked overtime to ensure that Manuel could stay in school.

Manuel studied hard and graduated as valedictorian, securing a full-ride scholarship to the local university where he planned to major in business, vowing to never live in poverty again.

However, sometime during Manuel's junior year of high school, God had come knocking. Manuel knew that God was calling him to be a pastor. Yet God's call did not fit what Manuel had always felt was his destiny. For Manuel, it was a decision of loyalties—would he choose to obey what God wanted, or would he choose his own way?

Our last example comes from the life of a girl named Tricia. Tricia came from a wealthy Christian family and had never wanted for anything. She was now a senior in college majoring in elementary education. Her plans were to take a position at the same elementary school that she had attended.

During Christmas break, Tricia attended a conference on missions where she heard speakers from a variety of countries describe the needs of their country. Each speaker urged volunteers to bring their skills to their countries—chief among those needs was education.

Wanting to learn more, Tricia read Henri Nowen's book *Compassion* and discovered what it meant to join God in His work in the world. Anxious to do that, she signed up for a mission trip to Guatemala over spring break. While there, Tricia felt God asking her if she would be willing to give her life to teaching these children. She eagerly said yes.

However, the excitement Tricia experienced was soon squashed by her parents' cold reaction to her plan. In short, they told Tricia that if she wanted to waste her life on those who were down and out, the marginalized of the world, that was her right. But she needed to know that they would not support her in this—financially, emotionally, or in any other way. As Tricia and I talked, it was apparent that she was wrestling with where her loyalties lay. Would she choose to follow God's direction and in so doing disappoint her parents, risking the possibility of being shunned by those who had cared for and nurtured her? Or would she choose the safety net of her parents, choosing to do what they expected of her, and in so doing turn her back on what she believed was God's plan for her life?

Each of these stories demonstrates a real-life choice that a person had to make regarding whom they would give their loyalty to. All of us have to make decisions, often on a daily basis, about whom we will serve and to whom we will give our loyalty.

Scripture gives us two great examples of this issue of loyalty and its importance for being holy people. One comes from the Old Testament; the other comes from the New Testament. Let's look at each of them in turn.

AN OLD TESTAMENT EXAMPLE

All throughout the Old Testament, we find that God's chosen people, the nation of Israel, struggled with this issue of loyalty. Repeatedly, Israel found itself waffling back and forth between following their God (the Creator who had revealed himself to them) and following the gods of the people around them. One story in particular readily illustrates this conflict of loyalties. It is found in 1 Kings 17-18. Let me encourage you to read these two chapters now.

King Ahab and Queen Jezebel had convinced the Israelites to follow a false god named Baal rather than the one true Creator God (who called himself "Yahweh," which was very close to the word for "I AM"). Because of this, God sent Elijah to proclaim to them that "As the LORD, the God of Israel, lives, whom I serve, there will be neither dew nor rain in the next few years except at my word" (1 Kings 17:1). That way, when God restored rain to the land, they would know it was from Him and not from the false god Baal.

In the middle of this three-year drought, God sends Elijah to confront Ahab and to clean house before He sends rain. Elijah makes it clear that Ahab has brought the drought upon the children of Israel by encouraging their idolatry! The Lord Almighty had been rejected in favor of weak, anemic, false gods! The drought serves as a warning that the result of false worship is not only physical dryness and lacking, but spiritual dryness as well.

Despite the fact that the rain is coming and the land of Samaria will soon be budding with new life, Elijah recognizes that if the people remain in their sin, they will continue to be barren spiritually. Therefore, he sets up an incredible confrontation. Elijah calls all the prophets of Baal to Mount Carmel for a final showdown in full view of the people. In a moment of great faith, the Lord gives Elijah the strength to ask the people a soul-piercing question: "'How long will you waver between two opinions? If the LORD is God, follow him; but if Baal is God, follow him'" (1 Kings 18:21). In short he was saying, "Make up your mind! Where do your loyalties really lie? With the true God, or the impostor?"

Did you notice the people's response? They say absolutely, positively nothing! They have been confused by the claims of the false gods for so long that they are unable to decide. You see, they want to have it both ways—to be able to worship both God and Baal. As a result, they walk with one foot for the Lord and one foot for Baal. However, their steps are clumsy and awkward because of the fundamentally different directions of the two religions. God calls them to become "a kingdom of priests and a holy nation" (Exodus 19:6), seeking to live in obedience while sharing the love of God with others. Baal invites them to a life of self-indulgence where everything revolves around self-gratification, especially through satisfying their own sexual desires.

The Israelites are so oblivious to their sin that something drastic must be done. The Lord is demanding a decision from them. To continue to limp along undecided is in effect to choose to dance with Baal's prophets. By refusing to choose until this point, the people had chosen Baal by default. So, Elijah sets the stage and issues a challenge: let each side prepare an altar and a sacrifice, without a fire. "The god who answers by fire—he is God" (1 Kings 18:24).

The Baal worshipers go first. They call upon their god from morning 'til night with no response. The sacrifice is untouched. The drought remains. So they dance harder and cut their flesh in an effort to appease their god. Elijah stands nearby watching this spectacle unfold, and he can't help taunting the Baal worshipers. "Shout louder! Maybe your God is asleep! Shout louder! Perhaps he is deep in thought! Shout louder! Maybe your God is in the restroom" (1 Kings 18:27, author's paraphrase)! The prophets of Baal continue their frantic dancing and yelling until evening. However, nothing happens.

Baal has not answered the prayers of his followers. Will this God known as "Yahweh" be able to do any better? Elijah reminds the people of their identity as God's people by building an altar with 12 stones representative of the 12 tribes of Israel, and he dedicates the altar to God. The offering is then placed on the altar. Elijah starts digging a trench around the altar; he then orders that 4 large jars of water be poured on the sacrifice—3 times. After the last jar has been poured on, Elijah confidently calls upon his Lord.

As Elijah finishes praying, suddenly a huge ball of flame falls from heaven and consumes the sacrifice, the wood, the stones, the soil, even the water. As the fire of Yahweh fell, so the people fell. They are no longer silent witnesses; they fall to the ground exclaiming, "'The LORD—he is God! The LORD—he is God'" (1 Kings 18:39)! With this confession, the way is cleared for the ending of the drought without any question as to who was responsible for it. Yahweh has once again magnificently shown himself to be the only true God, the only One worthy of our loyalty.

AN EXAMPLE FROM THE NEW TESTAMENT

The New Testament story is found in Mark 10:17-31. Take some time to read through this passage.

Jesus had spoken to hundreds, perhaps thousands of people that morning. He then traveled to Judea on the other side of the Jordan River. There, He had healed those brought to Him, as well as engaged in a verbal battle of wits with the Pharisees. Parents then began bringing their children to Jesus, asking Him to bless them. The disciples, missing the point entirely, intervened, trying to stop this waste of the Master's time. However, Jesus helped them realize that the kingdom of heaven is very much about little ones like this, and the type of faith these children have.

So imagine how tired Jesus was when a young man approached Him. This young man would have been well fed, well dressed, and perhaps even traveled with an entourage. But as he approached Jesus, he was sincere, seeking to find the answer to his question: "What must I do to inherit eternal life?" (v. 17).

Jesus pointed out that the young man already knew the commandments. He just needed to follow them. I'm sure that at Jesus' response, the young man's spirits were lifted. He had lived an exemplary life and was meticulously obedient to all the commandments. So if all that is required is to obey the commandments, then he was in. Eternal life was his.

But with Jesus, we see that the life of holiness—the life of perfection—entails more than obedience. Obedience alone is not enough, Jesus says. "If you want to be perfect, go, sell your possessions and give to the poor, and you will have treasure in heaven. Then come, follow me" (Matthew 19:21).

At Jesus' words, the young man's world started crumbling. He built his entire life around doing the things he thought were right, only now to be told that wasn't enough. Why would Jesus ask so much of this young man? Did He really mean for the rich young man to give up everything he owned? Isn't that going a bit too far?

Jesus identified a struggle of loyalty in the rich man's life. The rich young man came looking for eternal life. But when Jesus told him that his quest for perfection would cost him all of his possessions, he struggled with this decision, eventually walking away, unwilling to pay such an enormous price. What the rich young man failed to learn that day was that along with obedience to God comes self-denial. There can be nothing between us and God.

Notice that Jesus is not saying the young man must give away his possessions for the sake of the poor. He must give them away for his *own* sake—for the sake of holiness—for the sake of his soul. As long as he could fall back on his riches to sustain him, he would never have to learn to fully rely on God alone for his life.

Like the rich young man, you and I must also renounce those things which keep us from depending on anything other than God. The invitation of Jesus to holiness, to perfection (He says to the young man, "if you want to be perfect . . ."), is an invitation to give up everything—and anything—to follow Him. In a very real sense, what the story of the rich young man tells us is that holiness is a form of nakedness. In other words, absolutely nothing is to stand between us and God. This type of dependence demonstrates where our ultimate loyalties lie. Martin Luther, the founder of Protestantism, once remarked that "where your heart is, and where your security is, that has become your God."

OUR OWN FALSE GODS

What we have seen in these two stories is a deep conflict in religious loyalties. Each story shows us that we can't limp along with two different opinions, hobbling with one foot on the path of "Baal" and the other on the path of God; one foot wrapped up in the security of the world and the other stepping out into the risky unknown of following God. As much as we'd like to think so, this problem with loyalty is not just relegated to Israel or the rich young man. Throughout human history, we have been incredibly good at rationalizing what we do. We have learned to take the most extraordinary sets of opposite beliefs, values, and practices and make them appear compatible, and even look necessary to each other. For example, I knew of one young lady who had accepted Christ but continued to practice her Wiccan religion as well. She didn't seem to recognize the incompatibility of these two religions. Jesus spoke to this saying that no one can serve two masters (Matthew 6:24) but for some strange reason we keep trying and hoping. We refuse to choose because we enjoy playing both ends against the middle, trying to enjoy the best of both worlds.

The story of Elijah and the prophets of Baal would be even more powerful if the people of Israel had used this episode to align their loyalties once and for all. However, we find that a couple of generations later, Baal is back (see 2 Kings 10:18–28). Almost a hundred years later, during the lifetime of the prophet Hosea, many Israelites were still (or again) worshiping Baal instead of or alongside of Yahweh (see Hosea especially chapters 1-2). And in the story of the rich young ruler, the decision wasn't between Yahweh and Baal, but the loyalty issue is still present—will the young man continue to trust in his wealth or in the God who provided the wealth?

My point here is twofold. First, this issue of loyalty goes back all the way to Adam and Eve when they chose to follow their own will instead of God's. Second, all throughout Israelite's history, they continued to struggle with the issue of loyalty. One would assume that after God's phenomenal display of power over Baal, the people of Israel would have made up their minds once and for all. The problem is that the Israelites, like us, have short memories. As a result, we find them going back to this false god time and time again.

We need to ask ourselves, "Where are we wavering between two loyalties?" What form does our drought take? What are the various "Baals" that we are trying to embrace in our relationship with Christ that have no business being there? What are the things which would make us go away sad if Jesus asked us to give them up? Like the Israelites and the rich young man, God is calling us to abandon all our false gods—all the things that we depend on more than God—and learn to rely totally on Him. God passionately desires our undivided heart. In fact, He won't accept anything less than everything.

MAKING THE CHOICE

Like the Israelites or the rich young man, so often we refuse to give up those things of lesser value so that we may receive that which is of greatest value. In C. S. Lewis's book *The Great Divorce,* he tells a story about a man and a red lizard that lives on his shoulder.[7] The lizard is a metaphor, representing the lust the man has in his life. An angel comes to the man wanting to kill the lizard, but the man is reluctant to let the angel kill it. However, when he finally allows the angel to kill it, the lizard is transformed into a beautiful horse. What Lewis intends by this parable is to show us that sin is a paltry shadow of real truth, beauty and goodness, and that what God wants to give us is far more glorious and wonderful than the poor substitutes to which we cling.

Some of us refuse to make the choice, afraid of what it will cost us.

Maybe our trouble lies in our refusal to make choices of any kind, trying to hide from God's demand for commitment behind the screen of noninvolvement, apathy, or the daily struggle of life. The New Testament reflects a similar distaste for a lukewarm response to God's call (see Revelation 3:16). Our divided heart becomes dry spiritually, and we walk away sad when we attempt to share our heart with something other than God. God is calling us to an undivided belief in Him. But that belief must produce action, and that action results in a committed, consistent lifestyle.

So the question is: Have you given Christ your undivided loyalty? Have you made the decision that nothing else is as important as following Christ, regardless of how alluring it may appear? Have you decided that if Christ asks you to give something up in order to follow Him that it will be worth the cost?

When we elect to give ourselves totally to God, what we discover is that everything we might have given up suddenly pales in comparison to following God. Consider the case of Paul. He was a man who was extremely well educated, a man of both Jewish and Roman citizenry, someone who benefited from the best society had to offer him. In Philippians 3:4-6 Paul describes all the things he had going for him; he makes it clear to his readers that when it comes to being religious, he's at the top of the class.

Yet, when Paul encountered Christ on the way to Damascus, his life was forever changed. All of those things which at one time had seemed so important were now viewed as worthless in comparison to knowing Christ. In fact, Paul says:

But whatever was to my profit I now consider loss for the sake of Christ. What is more, I consider everything a loss compared to the surpassing greatness of knowing Christ Jesus my Lord, for whose sake I have lost all things. I consider them rubbish, that I may gain Christ and be found in him, not having a righteousness of my own that comes from the law, but that which is through faith in Christ—the righteousness that comes from God and is by faith. I want to know Christ and the power of his resurrection and the fellowship of sharing in his sufferings, becoming like him in his death, and so, somehow, to attain to the resurrection from the dead (Philippians 3:7-11).

Paul powerfully demonstrates that when we fully give of ourselves to Christ and allow Him to show us all that He has to offer us, nothing else will matter except for "the surpassing greatness of knowing Christ Jesus" (v. 8) as our Lord and Savior.

A student once wanted to know how to gain wisdom and insight, so he went to the wisest man in the town, Socrates, to seek his counsel. Socrates, being a man of few words, chose not to speak but to illustrate.

He took the student to the beach and walked straight into the water—clothes and all. Once the student joined Socrates in the water, Socrates turned to the student and pushed him under.

While the Socrates held him under the water, the boy struggled to get free—to survive. Just before life was taken away, Socrates released him. After gasping in air, the boy waded to the beach where Socrates now was and shouted, "Why did you try to kill me?"

Socrates calmly answered with a question, "When you were underneath the water, not sure if you would live or die, what did you want more than anything in the world?"

The student thought for a few moments, then softly said, "I wanted to breathe."

Socrates looked at the boy and said, "Ah! When you want wisdom and insight as badly as you wanted to breathe, it is then that you shall have it."[8]

When we desire Jesus in this way, when we are able to fix our eyes solely on Him, giving Him our total allegiance and undivided loyalty, and relinquishing those things which would keep us from being totally dependent on God, then we will truly know what it means to be holy people.

Questions to Ponder

1. What does it mean to give someone else our loyalty or allegiance?
2. Which of the two biblical characters did you identify with more: the Israelites who were walking the fence trying to serve both God and Baal, or the rich young man who was unwilling to give up those things which were most important to him in order to serve God?

Feelings to Process

1. What are some of the other loyalties you have in your life besides God? Why do you continue to give your loyalty to them, even while knowing that God wants all of our allegiance?
2. In Psalm 42:1, the Psalmist David writes: "As the deer pants for streams of water, so my soul pants for you, O God." An important part of enjoying the freedom God offers is developing a greater de-

sire to serve God than to indulge in our sin. Can you truthfully say that you desire God more than your sin? What does it feel like to desire God more than the very air that you breathe?

Actions to Practice

1. Consider what cheap, imitation treasures you are holding on to (like the red lizard), and as a result, missing out on the beautiful extravagance that God has to offer. Write out a list of those things. Offer the list to God as an offering and allow Him to give you what He's been anxiously waiting to offer.

2. Pray this prayer each evening for the next week: "Father, I want to serve You but there are so many things that vie for my attention. Give me blinders so I can focus exclusively on You. Instill in me a deep desire to want You more than anything else in this world. And help me learn that nothing else can compare with Your Holy Love for me. Amen."

CHAPTER 3
BREAKING THE CHAINS
EXPERIENCING
LIBERATION FROM SIN

*"I cannot, by direct moral effort, give myself new motives.
After the first few steps in the Christian life we realise [sic]
that everything which really needs to be done in our souls can
be done only by God."*—C. S. Lewis, Mere Christianity

When we first gave our lives to Jesus, something phenomenal occurred. We encountered a peace unlike anything we had ever known. There was a sense of purity that had not been present before and an overwhelming sense that all was right with the world. Jesus had forgiven our sins, washed us clean with His blood, and we now lived in relationship with Him.

However, it wasn't long before we quickly realized that there was still something wrong with us. We really wanted to serve Jesus, and most of the time we did it well. The problem was that there were other times when we would fall prey to some of the same old sins for which Christ had forgiven us.

MY STRUGGLE

When I was in high school, I had my first encounter with pornography at a friend's house. My friend had bought a pornographic magazine. He thought he was so mature in looking at it, and he invited me to participate. I have to admit that while I initially resisted, the temptation was strong, and I soon found myself eagerly devouring the magazine with him. That event soon turned into another at another friend's house, and it wasn't long before I found myself caught up in the sin of pornography.

Even though I was at best a nominal Christian during those years, I knew that pornography was wrong, so every time I would indulge in a pornographic magazine (this was in the days before the internet), I felt guilty and deeply ashamed afterward for what I had done. I would confess my sin to God, asking Him for forgiveness and cleansing, and promise not to participate in this sin again. Assured of God's forgiveness, I would plunge ahead, doing well for several days or even weeks, until the next opportunity arose and I once again fell to the allure of temptation. And once again, I would repeat the process of asking for God's forgiveness, seeking His cleansing, and promising not to engage in that activity ever again. This cycle repeated itself in my life hundreds of times during my high school days. Dismayed by my inability to stop, I even began praying that God would take away my sexual appetite. (Looking back now as a happily married man, I'm glad that God didn't answer my prayer, but then it seemed like the only solution.) Nothing seemed to be working.

While in college, I confessed to a friend my addiction, and he suggested that I talk to one of my professors. Through his friendship, care, and spiritual guidance over the next year, I slowly realized that I was still bound by the chains of sin. Yes, I had asked Jesus to forgive me of my sins, time after time after time, but I was still captive by my seeming inability to stop sinning.

My professor suggested that I read something the apostle Paul wrote to the Roman church about this very issue:

> For if I know the law but still can't keep it, and if the power of sin within me keeps sabotaging my best intentions, I obviously need help! I realize that I don't have what it takes. I can will it, but I can't do it. I decided to do good, but I don't really do it; I decided not to do bad, but then I do it anyway. My decisions, such as they are, don't result in actions. Something has gone wrong deep within me and gets the better of me every time.
>
> It happens so regularly that it's predictable. The moment I decide to do good, sin is there to trip me up. I truly delight in God's commands, but it's pretty obvious that not all of me joins in that delight. Parts of me covertly rebel, and just when I least expect it, they take charge. I've tried everything and nothing helps. I'm at the end of my rope. Is there no one who can do anything for me? Isn't that the real question? (Romans 7:17-24, TM).

Go back and reread those words. You may have felt that way in your own life. It seems as if the writer, Paul himself, the greatest missionary and theologian the church has ever known, wrestled in the same way that I wrestled—he knew the good he should do and the sin he should avoid, and he eagerly desired to follow the right path, but something kept him from being able to follow through.

THE ORIGIN OF OUR SIN NATURE

This tendency toward sin is obvious in children. You don't have to teach a child to lie; most of the time it's a struggle to teach a youngster to tell the truth. You will never struggle to teach a child to be selfish; the challenge will be to teach a child to share. You will not have to teach a child to disobey; it is respect for authority that must be instilled. That is because each of us enters this world with a heart that is bent toward evil. We are born separated from God, living under the power of sin.

All of us are under this curse. We want to serve Christ, we don't want to give in to temptation, and yet we do. In some ways it almost seems as if it is beyond our control. No matter how hard we try to resist, we simply can't do it.

And that, of course, is the issue. Because of Adam and Eve's sin, all of us have this tendency to self-rule. We want to be in charge, doing what we want, when we want it, where we want it, and how we want it. In a sense, each of us relives the fall of Adam and Eve. In the books of Romans and Galatians, Paul explains that all humans, along with all creation, are trapped in a slavery from which we are entirely unable to free ourselves. We are predisposed to sin—inclined to do it. Without outside help, our general tendency is to sin. It is as if we are born slaves, and sin is like an evil tyrant who holds us captive. It rules over our lives so powerfully that we are helpless to resist it by ourselves.

While individual acts of sin may no longer be paramount in our lives, there is still an issue of absolute rule at stake. At its very core, this sinful tendency we have is self-love. It is our belief that we know best, that we should be in charge. The question at stake is this: How much of my life am I willing to allow God to have? This is what theologians refer to as our sin nature. It is the curse that all of humanity is under due to Adam and Eve's rebellion against God. By ourselves, we are helpless against it. No matter how hard we try to do good, we can't, as long as we are under the influence of our sinful nature.

All of us, I'm convinced, long to be released, to experience the freedom that Jesus, through the Holy Spirit, offers us. The real question is how do we do this? How do we escape the chains of sin that bind us and enjoy the liberation that is available?

FREE OR CHAINED?

It's a terrible thing to have the opportunity to be free and not choose to accept it, preferring to live in bondage. Whether it's due to fear of the unknown, an unwillingness to give up those things we consider important, or simply a failure to understand that freedom is indeed possible, it's a terrible thing to have the opportunity to be free and yet remain bound in servitude.

That's true spiritually too; when Jesus Christ saved you, He made you free (John 8:36). Therefore, one purpose of the Holy Spirit's ministry is to help us experience the freedom Jesus purchased for us. We need this even as believers because some of us are trapped and held hostage by all manners of things. But that is not the way God intended for us to live. Listen to Paul's word to the Galatians: "Christ has set us free to live a free life. So take your stand! Never again let anyone put a harness of slavery on you" (Galatians 5:1, TM). So what is it that keeps us harnessed to a yoke of slavery?

Some of us are trapped in our past. Things that happened a long time ago still control how we function today. Others of us are bound by our fears, insecurities, and worries. We spend so much time worrying about what might happen that we never get around to enjoying what is happening. Still others of us are worried by what those around us think, trying to live how they think we should live, and in the process fail to be the unique people God created us to be.

We could expand this list indefinitely, but let's get to the good news. No matter what form of slavery you may be under, you can be liberated because the Holy Spirit is the Great Emancipator ("one who sets slaves free"). His job is to set you free, to release you from those things that hold you hostage, so that you can enjoy all that God has to offer you.

Now let's be careful here—freedom never means you are free to do whatever you want. That's license. Freedom means that God has liberated you to fulfill the purposes for which He has saved you. Think about it. Jesus Christ looked down through history, saw you trapped in sin and death, and gave His life to save *you* and set you free.

OLD HABITS ARE HARD TO BREAK

But like a prisoner with a life sentence, we have gotten used to being locked up in our cell of sin all these years. We have been bound in old relationships and old dependencies and old habits so long that when the Holy Spirit comes to set us free, we don't know how to respond. Instead we just keep doing the same old things we used to do because we are not used to freedom.

Author Chuck Swindoll tells a story about a market that was held in a village in northern India. One old farmer brought in a whole flock of quail to sell. He had tied a string around one leg of each bird; the other ends he tied to a ring, which loosely fit over a central stick. With one leg tied, the quail learned to walk in a circle around the stick. Nobody seemed interested in buying the birds until a religious man of high standing came along. His heart of compassion went out to those poor little creatures walking in their monotonous circles.

"I want to buy them all," he told the merchant, who was elated. After receiving the money, he was surprised to hear the buyer say, "Now, I want you to set them all free." The farmer was shocked. "You heard me. Cut the strings from their legs and turn them loose. Set them all free!"

With a shrug, the old farmer bent down and snipped the strings off the quail. They were freed at last. But the birds simply continued marching around and around in a circle. Finally, the man had to shoo them off. But even when they landed some distance away, they resumed their predictable march. Free, unfettered, released . . . yet they kept going around in circles as if still tied.[9]

Unfortunately, that's the way that too many Christians live their lives. When we accepted the forgiveness of Jesus Christ, we were given freedom: freedom from our sins and freedom from death. We knew that Christ had redeemed us, and we would live eternally in heaven. But in response, many Christians would just go around and around in a cycle of returning to sin.

But that is *not* the entirety of the freedom that Christ came to give us. Another part of the freedom that the Spirit offers is a release from the things that bind us, including our *carnality*. That word means, "living by the sinful desires of our flesh." The Scriptures often refer to this as the flesh, our sinful nature, and even the "old man." Now don't misunderstand. When we say "flesh" that doesn't mean our physical bodies and our physical desires are evil in themselves. When Scripture talks about the flesh, it is talking about our bodies and appetites under the destructive control of our old nature inherited from Adam and thoroughly ruined by sin.

Confession time. In one of the jobs I held, I had the opportunity to travel, speak, train others, and be engaged in some high-level meetings with some of the big names in youth ministry. I have to admit that I really liked this job, as it fed my ego and made me think that I was really somebody important. This was especially true during an interim period when my boss had left to take another assignment, and I had the opportunity to take over some of his responsibilities. This just reinforced in my mind that I was somebody pretty important and that I was right where I needed to be.

As we began the search for a new boss, there were several candidates who were promising, but one in particular caught my eye. This person had the background necessary to lead us in the direction we were headed and was someone I considered a friend. I just knew that we would work well together and was elated when I found out he had accepted the position. I was really looking forward to our partnership together.

However, my excitement was short-lived. My new boss did indeed have the vision and drive to take us where we needed to go. The problem was that in order for us to go there, he asked me to take a different position, one which would necessitate me giving up a lot of the things I was doing (and which I really enjoyed), so I could spend my time focusing on those things which were more important to the new direction of our department.

I hate to admit it, but I balked. In fact, I outright rebelled against my boss, choosing to undermine his authority rather than support him. You see, as much as I liked my boss personally, and even though I had supported his coming and the direction in which we had to move, in the end I was selfish, unwilling to give up what I was doing, so I could be involved in something even greater from the organization's perspective. You see, I liked being in control, and I didn't want to give it up.

That is a perfect description of our flesh. It doesn't want to give up control. But when we ask Jesus into our lives, He's now in charge. If we let the "I'm in charge" attitude stick around, we will always be in spiritual exile and will never enjoy the privilege of truly being free. We will only be free when we recognize that there is another, surpassingly great, power at work in our lives—the Holy Spirit—and yield ourselves to His control.

Scripture, however, tells us that we don't have to stay chained up by sin. Paul understood this well when he wrote, "Therefore, there is now no condemnation for those who are in Christ Jesus, because through Christ

Jesus the law of the Spirit of life set me free from the law of sin and death. For what the law was powerless to do in that it was weakened by the sinful nature, God did by sending his own Son in the likeness of sinful man to be a sin offering" (Romans 8:1-3a). The power of Christ through the ministry of the Holy Spirit can free us from the sins of the flesh. Jesus alone was able to take our sin upon himself, and through His triumphant resurrection from the dead, declare our sin dead once and for all. Because of Jesus, we have been set free from sin. He did for us what we could not do for ourselves.

NO LONGER SLAVES

But freeing us from sin is not all that has been done for us through Christ, by the power of the Spirit. Not only does the Spirit free us from the things that bind us, but He also frees us to be what God had intended us to be. In fact, by sending the Holy Spirit, Christ wanted us to experience a level of freedom that we could never have imagined. It was the freedom to be like Him: "Be holy, because I am holy" (1 Peter 1:16). We are called to be the body of Christ in the world. This happens as we show forth love, as we practice holy living, and as we seek to become more like Christ in word, thought, and deed. But it does not happen in our own power. It comes through the power of the indwelling Spirit in our lives. For us to be free in Christ, we must learn to rely upon the power that the Holy Spirit brings to our lives.

Allowing the Holy Spirit to come into our lives and be in charge is a big step, because letting someone else be in charge of our lives is a hard decision to make. You see, when we've been in charge for so long, it's not an easy transition to suddenly let someone else be in control. To do so means that we have to be able to pray with Jesus, "Not my will, but yours be done" (Luke 22:42). This is not easy, for our natural instinct is to follow what we desire, what we think is best for us. In my opinion, the biggest barrier to being able to pray this prayer is that we do not really believe God is good and knows what is best for us. Like Eve in the Garden of Eden, we think He is holding out on us, that the things He forbids will make us happy or improve our lives. Until we really believe that God is perfectly good and perfectly wise, we will not want to be holy. When we really believe that, we will want to be holy more than anything else in this world, because we will see that it is the only way to true happiness and fulfillment.

However, it is important to recognize that when we say no to the self, it must be for no other purpose than that of saying yes to God. Otherwise, it is too easy to default into a "works righteousness"—feeling that we have to continually earn God's favor by what we do or don't do—or to begin feeling prideful for our self-restraint in not participating in sinful things. Instead, the things we choose to participate in should always be undertaken for the love of God; for the things that motivate us, at least in part, also determine our allegiance. Author and teacher Robin Maas brilliantly explains this idea: "What looks initially like a battle between raw human will and overpowering temptation must eventually be understood as . . . an invitation to trust God's grace rather than our own strength of character."[10]

When God bought us with His blood, it was for a specific reason. Perhaps this story will help you better understand this idea. As I recall, back in the 1800s, a young man from England traveled to California. Like many others of that day, he was in search of gold. The young man staked a claim for a small area, and finally, after several months of prospecting, he struck it rich. He dug up all the gold that was there, and then decided to call it quits. As he began the long journey back to his home, he made a stop in New Orleans.

The young man hadn't been in the city very long when he stumbled upon a crowd of people. He noticed that they all seemed to be staring in the same direction, so he was curious what they were looking at. As he approached the crowd, he quickly recognized that the people were gathered to participate in a slave auction. While slavery had been outlawed in England for years, it was still alive and well in many states in the United States. The young man was extremely curious why people would choose to engage in such a deplorable practice, so he pushed his way to the front of the crowd in an effort to see this spectacle up close and personal. Just as he got to the front, he heard "Sold!" and watched forlornly as a middle-aged black man was taken away.

Next up was a beautiful young black girl. She was pushed up onto the platform and made to walk around so everyone could see her. The young man could hear the vile jokes and comments that the men around him uttered, things which spoke to how these evil men intended to use this young girl. Many of the men were even laughing as they gazed lustily on this new item for sale.

The bidding began.

Immediately the bids shot up, quickly surpassing what most slave owners would ever consider paying for a black girl. As the bids continued their upward climb, it quickly became apparent to the young miner that there were two men who wanted her. In between their bids, they laughed about what they were going to do with her, and how the other one would miss out. The young miner stood silent, his face set and determined, his entire body shaking with the anger that welled up inside of him. Finally, one man bid a price that was beyond the reach of the other. The girl looked down. The auctioneer called out, "Going once! Going twice!"

But just before the final call, just before the young girl was bought and sold to the man with the evil intentions, the young miner yelled out a price that was exactly twice the previous bid. In fact, it was an amount that exceeded the worth of any person—man, woman, or child. A few began to chuckle, and soon the entire crowd was laughing out loud. They assumed that the miner was only joking, wishing that he could be the one to have his way with the slave girl. However, the auctioneer motioned for the miner to come up and show his money. The miner jumped up on the platform, opened up the bag of gold he had brought for the trip, and showed it to the auctioneer. The auctioneer shook his head in disbelief as he waved the girl over to him.

The girl walked down the steps of the platform until she was eye-to-eye with the miner. Then, unexpectedly, she spat straight in his face and said through clenched teeth, "I hate you!" The miner, without a word, wiped his face, paid the auctioneer, took the girl by the hand, and walked away from the still-laughing crowd.

As they walked up and down the streets of that city, it seemed to the slave girl as if the young man was looking for something in particular, but what it was she did not have a clue. Finally they stopped in front of some sort of store, though the slave girl did not know what type of store it was. She waited irritably outside as the young miner went inside and started talking to an elderly man. While she couldn't make out what they were talking about, it was clear that there was some sort of disagreement, evidenced by their animated actions. At one point the voices got louder, and she overheard the store clerk say, "But it's the law! It's the law!" Peering in the store, she saw the miner pull out his bag of gold and empty it out on the table.

With what seemed to the slave girl like a look of disgust, the clerk reluctantly picked up the gold and went into a back room. Shortly thereafter, he came out with a piece of paper that both he and the miner signed.

As the miner came out the door, the slave girl intentionally looked away, not willing to give her new owner the satisfaction of seeing her face. The miner, however, stretched out his hand and said to the girl, "Here are your emancipation papers. You are free." The girl simply looked away, unwilling to even acknowledge what she perceived as her owner toying with her.

The young man tried once again. "Here. These papers say that you are now free. Take them."

"I hate you!" the girl said, refusing to look up. "Why do you make fun of me!"

"No, listen," the young man pleaded. "These are *your* freedom papers. I no longer own you. You are now a free person."

The girl looked at the papers, then looked at the miner, and looked at the papers once again. She seemed incredulous. "You just bought me . . . and now, you're setting me free?"

"That's why I bought you. I bought you to set you free."

The beautiful young girl immediately dropped to her knees in front of the miner, with tears streaming down her face. "You bought me to set me free! You bought me to set me free!" she said over and over.

Clutching his muddy boots, the girl looked up at the miner with new-found respect, admiration, and love and said, "All I want to do is to serve you—because you bought me."[11]

POSSIBLE TO LIVE WITHOUT SIN?

At one time we were all slaves to sin and to death. We were slaves to ourselves. But Christ came to redeem us—to pay for our freedom. He bought us with His own blood that we might be free: "For you know that it was not with perishable things such as silver or gold that you were redeemed . . . but with the precious blood of Christ, a lamb without blemish or defect" (1 Peter 1:18-19). This is the good news of the gospel—we don't have to live a life bound by the chains of sin.

Reread that last paragraph if you need to, but catch this idea. It is possible to live without sin! Christ makes it possible. No longer do we have to give in to our natural impulses, our sinful nature, or our self-will; for when we offer all of these things to God and allow the Holy Spirit to begin a spiritual reclamation project in our hearts, we will finally understand that we can live free as God intended us to be.

Questions to Ponder

1. Think about the things that may still hold you captive in life—past mistakes, insecurities, fear of someone else being in charge. I'm sure you can think of others. What would it take for you to be willing to allow Christ to break the chains of those things that bind you and fully set you free?

2. Allowing God to have full control of our lives can be a scary thing, especially when we've been in charge for so long. Think about why people may be reluctant to give Christ total control of their lives. Write down some of those reasons.

Feelings to Process

1. As you think about giving control of your life to Jesus, which of the following phrases best expresses how you feel?

    __ I can't wait to see what Jesus is going to do with me.

    __ I'm reluctant to allow Jesus to make the decisions I've always made.

    __ Give up control? No way!

    __ I feel like I'm back and forth—one day I give it up, the next I take it back.

2. Think about someone you know who has experienced the freedom from sin that Jesus offers us. How do you feel when you're around them? What is there about them that is different from other people?

Actions to Practice

1. Part of experiencing the freedom that Christ offers us is the willingness to give all areas of our life to God for Him to do with as He will. Take some time to create a list of those areas that you've been holding onto—those areas that you're reluctant to turn over to Him. Now take that list and offer it to God. Let Him know that this list is now His list and that you're no longer in charge. Experience the freedom that only comes when we rid ourselves of our own selfishness and trust instead in the goodness of God. Share your decision with a friend.

2. Commit to spending more time listening to God in prayer in the weeks ahead. Ask God to point out those areas that you may be (unknowingly) holding onto and which keep you from experiencing the full freedom that He offers. Consider using a journal to record

what God says to you. If you're willing to listen and obey, then over time you will be able to look back and see how your character has begun to change, so that you are more like God than you were. A journal can be a great source of encouragement to you of how much God is doing in your life.

SECTION 2

FREEDOM FOR GOD
HOLINESS AS LOVE

CHAPTER 4
THE PERFECT LOVE
RESPONDING IN OBEDIENCE

*"Holiness is not a luxury for the few; it is not just for some people.
It is meant for you and for me, for all of us. We have been created for
it. It is a simple duty, because if we learn to love, we learn to be holy."*
—Mother Teresa of Calcutta[12]

The idea of holiness can be frightening for most of us. Too often, the word carries with it images of rules, limitations, and all the "thou shalt nots" of Scripture. Unfortunately, some people have perpetuated this myth by preaching a very legalistic form of holiness—legalistic in the sense that they think the only way to be holy is to follow every rule to a "t" every moment. This form of holiness is more concerned with doing all the right things than with being the right person.

However, there is another way to understand holiness that is relational in its nature. While it is concerned with how we act, it sees our actions as the byproduct of our relationship with God. In other words, holiness is a love story. We cannot become more holy by virtue of the things we do (or don't do). We become holy because a loving God chooses to make us holy. For many of us, this is a radical idea. In this chapter we will explore what this holy God is like, discover what the love relationship He desires to have with us looks like. This will help us understand how that love relationship defines what holiness is, does, and looks like.

OUR HOLY GOD

If we are to really understand this call to holiness, we must first gain a true picture of who this holy God is. Toward that end, we will look at how God is portrayed throughout Scripture. As we do this, we will hopefully begin to capture a more complete sense of our holy and loving God. Understanding God will help us know what kind of holiness He expects from us.

In the Old Testament, God is often described as holy (see Leviticus 11:44-45; Joshua 24:19; 1 Samuel 2:2; and Psalm 99:5). The Hebrew word *qodesh*, translated as "holiness," comes from a root word which means "apart" or "separate." Therefore, one of the first things we learn about this holy God is that He is not like us. He is in a completely different category than anything or anyone else. One theologian, trying to get the flavor of this idea, described God as "Wholly Other."[13] No other god is like Him; therefore, God alone can command, "You shall have no other gods before me" (Exodus 20:3). God alone demands our exclusive loyalty and worship. Because He is holy, God is also a jealous God. He will not tolerate rivals, nor will He condone our attempts to serve Him alongside of other gods. Joshua makes this clear to Israel when he tells them, "He is a holy God; he is a jealous God." (Joshua 24:19).

Let's take a look at Exodus 3. Go ahead; read it. Moses' life was spared as an infant because God protected him; however, as is often the case, Moses grows up and takes things into his own hands, killing an Egyptian guard in the palace. Now, he is out in the desert tending the flocks of his father-in-law, Jethro. It's just another ordinary day . . . until God shows up.

A bush on fire captures Moses' attention. That was certainly possible under certain conditions in the desert under the hot sun. What is strange is that this one does not seem to be burning up. Curious, he ambles over to look at it.

As he nears, he hears the Creator God calling out to him. When Moses answers, God says, "'Do not come any closer. . . . Take off your sandals, for the place where you are standing is holy ground'" (v. 5). So Moses does the only thing he knows to do in the presence of such a holy being—he takes off his shoes and kneels down in worship.

Moses' encounter with God shows us that our response in the midst of such holiness should be humility, respect, and worship.

The second passage we'll examine closely is Isaiah 6:1-6. Again, take a moment to read it. In order to understand this passage, we need some background. Isaiah is a priest who finds himself in the midst of a major leadership transition, for the king has died. Unsure what the next step is, Isaiah does the only thing he knows to do—he goes to the Temple to worship.

While there, Isaiah has a most remarkable experience—a vision in which he encounters God. In this vision, Isaiah sees God "high and exalted" (v. 1) with angels flying around calling out "Holy, holy, holy is the LORD Almighty" (v. 3). This triple use of the word holy is a common Hebrew way of expressing not just that God alone is holy, but that He alone is absolutely holy. God is the source of holiness and holiness is the very essence of His being. Holiness is not just an attribute of God; rather it is who He is. In the same way that John says "God is love" (1 John 4:16), Isaiah says God is holy. God is perfect in His holiness; even the angels are impure compared to God and have to hide their faces from Him. Isaiah, of course, is far from being holy, and does the only thing he knows to do—he admits that he is a sinful human who has no hope to be in the presence of the holy, holy, holy God.

In response to Isaiah's confession, God directs one of the angels to bring a live coal from the altar of holiness and touch it to Isaiah's lips. This is a symbol of God's purifying act. In response to Isaiah's confession of his sin, God provides pardon, forgiveness, and cleansing; the relationship between God and Isaiah is restored. Isaiah's experience illustrates what is possible for us—we also will be cleansed and restored if we will allow ourselves to be confronted by the holiness of God, confess our sinfulness, and receive His cleansing.

SET APART

In the ancient world, one became holy (set apart) as one dedicated himself or herself to a particular god or goddess. The person then took on the qualities of the deity. For instance, if you were a sun god worshipper, you might lie out in the sun all day to get sun-tanned, trying to take on the tanned skin "radiance" of the sun. At least you would be a living display of the effects of the sun on your body.

In a similar way, the true Creator God calls us to be like Him—holy as He is holy. While God alone is holy, holy, holy, He can make us holy, even though it may only be a human version of it (a holy people like our God, but not holy, holy, holiest like God himself).[14] Because of God's decision to redeem humanity from our sin, when we choose to accept that free and gracious gift, we are choosing to come under God's ownership—set apart for His use. This is what enables us to fulfill God's command to "Be holy because I, the LORD your God, am holy" (Leviticus 19:2).

In the Gospel of John, chapter 1, John makes it clear that Jesus is God. As such, He is holy (or rather, Jesus is "holy, holy, holy"). In fact, it was Jesus' death on the cross which once and for all defined what holiness looks like—it looks like love. God's love and His holiness are so intertwined that they are virtually inseparable. His love and holiness are not simply characteristics that tell us *about* God. They *are* God. As God lives out what it means to be love and what it means to be holy, He also makes a tyrannical claim upon our very lives, claiming our obedience and trust, sanctifying us (making us holy) as we give Him complete control of our lives. Our ability to be holy, therefore, is based entirely on what God has done for us and the relationship He chooses to establish with us.

CHRISTIAN PERFECTION

So what does this holy relationship with Jesus look like? Scripture describes it in odd terms, talking about our *perfection.*

The obvious question is what does perfection mean? Dictionary.com defines "perfect" as: "entirely without any flaws, defects, or shortcomings."[15] Consider the ways we strive for perfection in various areas of our lives. Baseball pitchers seek to throw a perfect game (meaning no hits, walks, or runs given up), while baseball batters try to get a hit every time they come to bat. A musician aims for perfection in their performance, hitting all the notes exactly as they are written. Doctors aim to never make a mistake, knowing the consequences can be deadly if they do. We work really hard to make everything perfect in our relationship with our boyfriend or girlfriend to ensure that they continue to like us. As a student, you may desire to be perfect when it comes to taking tests or writing a paper, knowing that this perfection can result in scholarships!

Yet even with all the ways we strive for perfection, most Christians are very uncomfortable with the word *perfection;* if there is one area of life in which Christians are likely to steer clear of perfection, it is in our relationship with God. In fact, many are downright terrified of the concept of perfection, believing that they can never be perfect. Instead, we are quick to label ourselves "sinners." Here, more than any other area of life, we are ready to expect *less* of ourselves rather than more. But what if Scripture calls us to perfection in our relationship with God?

Can we really be perfect? After all, isn't it enough that we are simply good most of the time? In fact, I would guess that most of us would be thrilled if we were "perfect" 99 percent of the time! Consider the baseball or softball player who bats .990—he or she would be guaranteed to enter the Hall of Fame! Or consider your next chemistry or physics test—who wouldn't be ecstatic with a grade of 99 percent?

While this may seem fantastic or unreachable, consider what would happen if the following businesses were perfect *ONLY 99.9 percent* of the time:

- $761,900 would be spent in the next 12 months on tapes and compact discs that won't play.
- 1,314 phone calls would be misplaced by telecommunications services every minute.
- 107 incorrect medical procedures would be performed today.
- 12 babies would be given to the wrong parents every day.
- 14,208 defective personal computers would be shipped this year.
- 18,322 pieces of mail would be mishandled in the next hour.
- 20,000 incorrect drug prescriptions would be written in the next 12 months.
- 22,000 checks would be deducted from the wrong bank accounts in the next 60 minutes.
- 5,517,200 cases of soft drinks would be shipped flat this year.
- 880,000 credit cards would be produced with incorrect magnetic strips.[16]

Even when we are not perfect only 0.1 percent of the time, it can still have huge consequences.

Now think about your own life. What percentage of perfection would you apply to your life (remembering our definition of "no flaws, defects, or shortcomings")? Fifty percent? Seventy percent? For a select few among us, maybe even 85-90 percent? That would be exceptional, to be perfect in everything we do 90 percent of the time. I think most of us would jump at that possibility.

However, consider that when it comes to our perfection, even 99.9 percent perfection is not enough, for the Bible makes it clear that even if we only mess up *one time* we've already blown it, "for *all* have sinned and fall short of the glory of God" (Romans 3:23, emphasis added) and the consequences for this imperfection are more than just a few bad things happening: "For the wages of sin is *death*" (Romans 6:23*a*, emphasis added).

But there is good news. First, you already know that Jesus Christ came to forgive you of those past sins, those choices you and I made which made us less than perfect. When Jesus died on the cross and then was resurrected, He once and for all made it possible for our sins to be forgiven. Second, Jesus continues to offer His forgiveness when we recognize that we have stepped outside of His will, when we've chosen to do things which run counter to God's character, or when we choose not to engage in things which God would want us to do. When this happens, we can go to Jesus, ask for His forgiveness, commit to changing that area of our life, and move on.

However, even with this assurance of forgiveness, none of us are still 100 percent morally perfect. And yet, like Abraham, all of us are called to walk faithfully with our God and be perfect or "blameless" (Genesis 17:1).

UNDERSTANDING THE WORD

Before we get too hung up on the word "perfection," it would be helpful to really understand what it means and doesn't mean biblically and spiritually. To do so will necessitate that we have a brief word study.

In the Old Testament, the word commonly translated with the English word "perfect" is *tamim*. *Tamim* means whole, sound, and unblemished—as in the case of a sacrificial offering, which must be perfect. The Hebrew word for "perfect" is often translated as "blameless," "sincere," or "upright." Perfection is something ascribed to God, who defines perfection, but in the Bible, human beings can also be perfect. Job (Job 1:1), Noah (Genesis 6:9), and Abraham (Genesis 17:1) were all perfect—because they walked with God. Their perfection was based on their understanding of God's law and their proximity and complete openness to God. In other words, the people who were considered blameless and upright were not perfect based on who they were or what they did, but based on who they were *in relation to God*. This is the key—their relationship to God based on what God does for us!

A similar pattern emerges in the New Testament. Here the word "blameless" is often found. Like its Old Testament counterpart, the word doesn't mean that we are never without fault or mistake, but rather that before God, we are seen as blameless because our intentions are pure. Our aim, our deepest desire, is to have one and only one focus—God. Or as one philosopher put it, "Purity of heart is to will one thing—the Good."[17]

Our English word perfection comes from the Latin *perfectio* and carries with it the connotation of "absolute perfection" or "sinlessness." If that was the type of perfection the Scripture described, we'd all be in trouble. Fortunately, it's not. Instead, when the New Testament talks about perfection it uses the Greek word *teleios*. This comes from a root word that means to the "end" or the "intended purpose." So from the Greek language of the New Testament, a thing is perfect when it *does what it was intended to do*.

For example, I like to play softball. The glove that I use is one that

I've had for over 15 years. It is old and beaten up, I've had to replace the stitching at least twice, almost all of the original padding has been lost, and the leather has cracked in several places. Anyone looking at the glove would assume that it was a piece of junk. But you know what? When I am out on the field, the glove does what it was intended to do—it catches softballs. So from a Greek perspective, the glove is perfect because it does what it was created to do.

When the Bible talks about our perfection, it is reminding us that we need to do what we were created to do. And what is that? An expert in the law came up to Jesus and asked Him what the greatest commandment was. Jesus' answer was classic: "'Love the Lord your God with all your heart and with all your soul and with all your mind.' This is the first and greatest commandment. And the second is like it: 'Love your neighbor as yourself.' All the Law and the Prophets hang on these two commandments" (Matthew 22:37-40). Obviously, this is easier said than done. We've previously discussed the things which can keep us from giving God our total allegiance. And as we'll see later, it can be equally hard to love people in the way God commands. Yet, when we allow God to begin to make us holy people, He gives us the power to love the way that He loves.

It is clear then that perfection is what God expects from us, that this expectation is not impossible, and that our perfection has a lot to do with how much our focus is on God (which then enables us to resist sin).

Moses clearly believed it was possible to walk in this type of deep communion with God. Standing on the edge of the Promised Land, knowing that his time as their leader was at an end, Moses proceeded to offer the Israelites his final words of instruction and hope:

> Now what I am commanding you today is not too difficult for you or beyond your reach. It is not up in heaven, so that you have to ask, "Who will ascend into heaven to get it and proclaim it to us so we may obey it?" Nor is it beyond the sea, so that you have to ask, "Who will cross the sea to get it and proclaim it to us so we may obey it?" No, the word is very near you; it is in your mouth and in your heart so you may obey it.
>
> See, I set before you today life and prosperity, death and destruction. For I command you today to love the LORD your God, to walk in his ways, and to keep his commands, decrees and laws; then you will live and increase, and the LORD your God will bless you in the land you are entering to possess (Deuteronomy 30:11-14).

"Christian perfection" then is not only a biblically accurate term for what happens to us, it is the very call God places upon us. When we were first saved, a very real change occurred. We were different people, with a new outlook and a desire to serve God. As the Holy Spirit began to work in our lives, we began to sense that there were things present that kept us from fully following God. This is the sinful nature we inherited from Adam and Eve and which we discussed in the last chapter. It is this sin nature that drives us to be self-sufficient rather than God-dependent.

WHAT PERFECTION IS NOT

Perfection does not mean that we will never sin again nor that every single desire, thought, and purpose will always be good. While that would be ideal, it is not reality. We must remember that there is a distinction between perfection of *purpose* (our intention) and perfection of *performance* (how we put that intention into practice). "Christian perfection is salvation from sin—from its *power* or *dominion* in the new birth and its *root* (false self-centeredness) . . . but it is not sinlessness."[18] Even the best of us still fall well short of the only standard of sinlessness that matters—God's. So while our performance may fall short of what God intended, we should (and can) have perfection of purpose.

In Christian perfection our intent is cleansed, but we still have not been delivered from all the consequences of Adam and Eve's sin. We will still make mistakes because we are human. We will have to work to overcome lifelong prejudices. However, this does not give us permission to dismiss those actions. The important thing is how we respond when God brings the issue to our hearts and minds. The one who is entirely sanctified will seek forgiveness of the one they have offended, as well as from God. ("Sanctification" is an important word that we will talk about more as we go on. It means to be cleansed and set apart. For more on this term, keep reading and see the Glossary of Holiness Terms in the back of the book.)

So let us understand that being made perfect means we are made clean, and "sanctified," but it does not mean that we immediately change who we are. There may be sins still hidden from us, personal quirks and imperfections, or mistakes based on ignorance. These were not considered obstacles to perfection as the church understood it. Much of this type of human frailty was expected to remain with us to death. What does change through sanctification is "who is in control" and what our response will be because of His control.

REFINED LIKE SILVER

Still, we have to admit that the idea of being perfect seems daunting at best. Just how do we do this? Some people talk about going out to "find themselves." The early church understood that it was necessary instead to remold ourselves—particularly our self-centered will. Imagine a silversmith working hard to create a piece of beautiful jewelry. If, in the process of refining and shaping the silver, the artisan discovers an imperfection—a small bubble or impurity that mars the finished product—he or she will simply throw it back in the pot, letting it melt again, so that it can be reshaped.

As part of this reshaping and refining process, early Christians sought to become complete—perfect if you will—by engaging in a process of formation. This process involved participation in a series of practices and spiritual disciplines that were designed to help mold and shape who they were as individuals and as a community. Of course, if we are going to be shaped and molded, there must be something that we are seeking to be like, a model to which we must conform. For the early church there was no question what they were going to emulate—Jesus, God Incarnate. "The model governing the shaping was Jesus Christ. More particularly, it was Jesus Christ crucified: divine Love, sacrificing itself for the other— for the unredeemed."[19]

Think back to the silver artisan crafting jewelry. In my travels, I've had the rare opportunity to see one of these professionals at work. The lady silversmith I watched held a piece of silver over a fire and let it heat up. She explained that when refining silver, you need to hold the silver in the very middle of the fire—where the flames are hottest—so as to burn away all the impurities.

As I watched, I was reminded of something I had heard about silversmiths. "Is it true," I asked, "that you have to sit in front of the fire the entire time the silver is being refined?"

"Yes," she answered. "However, it's not enough that I just sit here and hold it. I also have to watch it very carefully, never taking my eyes off of it. You see, silver is fragile. It needs the fire to purify it; however, if it is left in the fire for even a minute too long, it will be destroyed by the flames. So it is vitally important that I never take my eyes off of it. When the time comes and the silver is perfected, I will know it because I've been watching all the impurities burn away."

When she said this, I remembered a passage from Malachi 3:3 that talks about the character of God—"He will sit as a refiner and purifier of silver." I saw a parallel that perhaps you've recognized as well. When God chooses to purify us, by necessity, He has to remove the impurities. Before Jesus can make us perfect, He first has to remove all of our imperfectness—all of our sinful pride, self-will, and predisposition to sinning. And He alone knows when that process is complete, for Jesus alone is the one who is ever present, always with His eye on us, making sure we are cleansed fully but not destroyed.

As the silversmith removed the piece of silver from the fire and dumped it into a pail of water, I asked her how she knew that the silver was finally ready for its intended use. She smiled and replied, "Oh, that's the easiest part of the job. I know it's perfect when I see my image reflected in it."

BECOMING CHRISTLIKE

Think about that for just a moment. In order to become the holy people God has called us to be—perfect, complete, and ready to do what we were created to do—Jesus *must* be reflected in our lives. Everything we do, every word we say, every thought we think must be a reflection of Jesus. Do you remember how we defined holiness in the first chapter? We said that holiness was Christlikeness. "Jesus is the gift of holiness. The God who is totally unlike us became like us in Jesus. We can see what holiness looks like and how holiness behaves by watching Jesus."[20]

When Jesus is reflected in our lives, we are Christlike—we are holy people. The great Mahatma Gandhi of India once said, "I am not a Christian because I've never met anyone like Jesus. If I did, maybe I'd become one." Think how our world would be different if each of us lived a Christlike life so that everyone we encountered saw not us, but Jesus.

Understand, please, that if Jesus is to be reflected in our lives, this means that we have an ongoing relationship with Him, one that continually pulls us closer to Him and His will for our lives. When we live close to God we are holy people.

NOT AN END BUT A BEGINNING

Too many people (perhaps you're one of them) have only heard holiness, (often described as "entire sanctification"), talked about as an event (sometimes called a crisis). "Get sanctified," the saying goes, "and your life will be forever changed. No more sin." While it is true that there is an element of completeness in what God does to us, there is also a very real sense that this is just the beginning! The Scriptures talk about sanctification both as a decisive event and an ongoing Christian walk. God is continually working in us to mold us into His image, to renew us, to make us more holy. This is not just an event that happens to us and then God's work is complete. Rather, we need to understand God's ongoing work for exactly what it is—a lifelong journey of love. Robin Maas explains this beautifully:

> The tendency, for most of us, is to imagine perfection as a kind of stasis—a final point or plateau, especially if we think of it in terms of completion or maturity—but this is a fundamental misunderstanding of what the church means by perfection. In the first place, scripture and tradition both assume that we are always moving either toward God or away from God . . . But if we are meant to become like a God who is limitless love, then there can be no limit to our love for God. In that sense, we are never finished, never complete in having "enough" love.[21]

Holiness is more like a journey than a destination. We will never be able to be finished growing in our ability to love—there is no ceiling on it. What we can do is eliminate other "lesser" loves that compete for our attention and pull us in directions away from growing deeper in the love of God. It is here that the battle begins.

A CLASH OF WILLS

As we grow closer to God, we soon discover a basic clash of wills—ours against God's. It could be that God is asking you to choose new friends, give up an activity, change your major, or start a new ministry. Perhaps He is asking you to spend more time in prayer, to digest His Word more regularly, or to befriend the kid that no one else will even talk to. You see, if we truly desire to be closer to God, to become more holy, it means that we will have to follow Jesus' example and be able to say, "Not my will, but yours be done" (Luke 22:42). When this happens, the clash of wills ends. We are concerned only with growing closer to God and are willing to give up or take on whatever is necessary to deepen that relationship.

This is the type of love that doesn't allow any competitors. It is a love that leaves no room for rebellion, selfish desire, divided loyalties, or even a static understanding of love. When we have this type of love for God, He alone becomes our passion, our vision, and our future.[22]

Once we've entered into this holy love relationship with Jesus, our entire worldview begins to change. No longer do we see things the way we did before. Instead, we now see things as Jesus sees things. We recognize when others are wounded, scared, and alone. We more easily sense when there are areas of our life which keep us from wholehearted devotion to God. And we begin to desire God more than anything else in the world.

When we develop this type of relationship with God, when His desires become our desires, when we allow Him to have complete control of our lives, then everything we say and do will be influenced by that relationship. It's kind of like putting on "Jesus-colored" glasses. It directly influences how we view everything. No longer do we see just a kid at school that is always picked on. Instead we see Jesus. It isn't just another homeless person we passed on our way out to eat. It's Jesus. The friend whose parents are going through a divorce and feels incredibly alone and afraid becomes Jesus to those of us in this holy love relationship. I think this is what Jesus had in mind when He related the parable of the sheep and goats found in Matthew 25:31-46. Jesus makes it clear that when we minister to anyone out of the love Jesus offers, we are in essence ministering to Him.

HOLINESS AS RELATIONSHIP

While our obedience is important, because our holiness is relational, simply following God's commands is not the sum total of what we are about. Instead, holiness entails a total commitment, the surrender of every last love that stands between us and our Creator. Since perfection is about being *like God* and being like God means *loving like God* (for God is love), this is the call we are given—to love others, including our enemies, the way God loves us. The love of enemies is an unnatural, selfless, sacrificial love. It does not promise us personal satisfaction or fulfillment.

In fact, we have to make a daily choice whether we will continue to pursue this love relationship with God.

Since it is a *relationship*, we must choose to continue it. Since it is a *love* relationship, God will not coerce us or force himself on us—not at the beginning or later. He draws us to oneness. Therefore, when we learn that something in our lives does not please Him, we must deal with it. That's a choice only we can make. Yet, we don't make the choice on our own. God lovingly leads us and empowers us to deepen the relationship He has established with us.[23]

I'm convinced that seeing holiness as a relational issue is absolutely critical. You see, I grew up in a time period where "being holy" was much more about following rules and regulations than about a relationship with the Father. In fact, many of these rules and regulations became the test to determine whether one was truly sanctified. It often seemed as if it was more important to abide by these legalistic standards than it was to have a vital, growing relationship with Jesus Christ.

LOVE OR LEGALISM?

The unfortunate thing is that far too often it is this legalistic expression of holiness with which most people are familiar. As a result, when I talk about holiness with my non-Christian friends, their first instinct is to duck and run—they see it as something to avoid instead of something beautiful.

I understand there are two basic components to holiness—our identity as being holy people (a holiness *given* to us by God, not earned by ourselves) and the ethical practices in which we engage (the practical expression of being holy). However, there are two ways of looking at this, sort of a "chicken or egg" conundrum—which comes first? Some people start with the ethical practices. We do these things (whatever they may be) because they express what it means to be a holy person. Of course, the logical implication is that we become holy people by doing holy things. And there is certainly some evidence that suggests that engaging in certain behaviors does affect our identity. However, it seems to me that our focus has become on what we can't do. Too often we become fixated on right beliefs, rights actions, and even right experiences as the test for being holy. This seems to me to be a perversion of what God intended for us when He said, "I am the LORD your God; consecrate yourselves and be holy, because I am holy . . ." (Leviticus 11:44-45). When we live in holy love with God, then our focus will be on the joy, peace, and aliveness that comes from being sanctified—set apart for Him.

John Wesley wrote a wonderful little book titled *A Plain Account of Christian Perfection*[24] in which he laid out his understanding of holiness. In recently rereading this book, I saw for the first time two distinct thoughts: (1) the clear way in which Wesley seems to define human behavior by lists of things that we have to do; and (2) the extent to which he finally lets go of trying to define holiness by what we do and instead focuses on seeing it as our loving response to God for what He has done for us. There are many churches that emphasize holiness and live in this tension. When we let go of this tension and land on one side or the other, it seems that it almost always results in legalism. I would suggest that in a postmodern world, if the church has to err on one side or the other, let it err on the side of love rather than rules.[25]

My friend Ron wrote about his own experience with rules and love recently: "I think I must have been one of the fortunate ones who avoided adolescent rebellion against the rules of the Church. Perhaps it was because the people of our church were so loving. The rules didn't seem burdensome or legalistic because the bonds of our community life were so strong. We were buoyed and supported in our common life. The rules were the expression of our common commitment to be a holy people. Love trumped legalism."[26]

Therefore, our obedience in action doesn't happen because we feel like we have to do these things. Neither should it be based on what others say we should do. Instead, it should be based solely on our love for God. If we say we love God, then we should naturally want to do the things that God would want. In a sense, our day-by-day, consistent obedience to God is our way of saying, "I love you."

When we say that we love God, it should naturally impact every single area of our lives. We can't compartmentalize our lives; our love for God should be something that absolutely pervades our guiding principles, priorities, and relationships. What God really wants to see is how our love for Him and His love for us guides our day-to-day life. While God loves to hear you and me sing songs of praise to Him as a way of showing our love, what God is more concerned about is us demonstrating our love for Him by the way we treat our friends, use our money, meet the needs of others, work to correct injustice in the world, and how we choose to keep His commandments. The true demonstration of our love for God is revealed in the way we obey Him daily.

Let me illustrate. Doug is a friend of mine. He has been a Christian for many years and grew up in a holiness denomination. However, Doug might have a difficult time fitting in your or my church because, you see, Doug likes to have an occasional glass of wine or a beer with his meal. In addition, Doug occasionally drops a few choice words when he is angry at the injustices he sees all around him. In fact, Doug has actually been asked to leave one church because of these issues. He tried really hard to fit in, but in the end decided he just wasn't willing to invest his time trying to follow all the rules this particular church had created to define holiness.

Please don't misunderstand me. I'm not arguing that Doug should be allowed to drink nor am I arguing that cursing is OK. These are issues that Doug has to answer to God for, and he is also under the community ethic of the local faith community he has chosen to join, which has the power to help shape him. (We'll talk more about the role of the community of faith in shaping our character in chapter six.)

Yet for all these "negatives" regarding Doug's holiness, Doug may well be the most passionate practitioner of holiness I know. He is readily engaged in acts of compassionate service to the homeless community, the homosexual community, and those gripped by drugs and alcohol. Doug dares to enter into their worlds, worlds that most of us willingly choose not to engage, because his understanding of a holy God leads him to the belief that to do anything less would be to deny who he is in relation to God. Doug's (and my) understanding of God calls for a transformation that challenges the difficult realities around us. Doug illustrates that it is more important that holiness be practiced in real life rather than just discussed in theory.

This is the point I want to make: Holiness isn't what you do or don't do. It's who you are. When we choose to engage in certain practices, it is for no other reason than the love relationship we have with Jesus as we seek to draw closer to Him, seeking to serve Him above all. When we do this, our starting point and focus changes. "Jesus leads us not to focus on rules but on love. In the absence of passionate love for God, the most perfect conformity to all the rules will count for nothing. If we choose to love God fully and passionately, we will want to please God, as all passionate believers do their beloved. Keeping appropriate rules of conduct will never be an issue."[27]

You see, we weren't freed simply to be free. Though we were freed from sin, we then became bound again—only this time we are bound to Christ for the sake of others. Paul spells it our beautifully in Romans 6:11-23:

> In the same way, count yourselves dead to sin but alive to God in Christ Jesus. Therefore do not let sin reign in your mortal body so that you obey its evil desires. Do not offer the parts of your body to sin, as instruments of wickedness, but *rather offer yourselves to God as those who have been brought from death to life; and offer the parts of your body to him as instruments of righteousness.* For sin shall not be your master, because you are not under the law, but under grace.
>
> What then? Shall we sin because we are not under law but under

grace? By no means! Don't you know that when you offer yourselves to someone to obey him as slaves, you are slaves to the one whom you obey—whether you are slaves to sin, which leads to death, or to obedience, which leads to righteousness? But thanks be to God that, though you used to be slaves to sin, you wholeheartedly obeyed the form of teaching to which you were entrusted. *You have been set free from sin and have become slaves to righteousness.*

I put this in human terms because you are weak in your natural selves. Just as you used to offer the parts of your body in slavery to impurity and to ever-increasing wickedness, so now *offer them in slavery to righteousness leading to holiness.* When you were slaves to sin, you were free from the control of righteousness. What benefit did you reap at that time from the things you are now ashamed of? Those things result in death! But now that *you have been set free from sin and have become slaves to God*, the benefit you reap leads to holiness, and the result is eternal life. For the wages of sin is death, but the gift of God is eternal life in Christ Jesus our Lord (emphasis added).

Life within the freed community is to be marked by love. But this love is not simply a matter of sentimentality. In fact, the freedom God gives calls those of us who have been liberated to resist those sinful forces which are anxious to take us back into slavery. Part of our sanctification, being set apart for God and His use, means that we learn to become like trees of righteousness, continually bearing fruit for God.

It is my humble prayer that we would all live the lives we were created to live—lives which learn to love as we reflect the love God has for us, and in so doing, become holy people.

Questions to Ponder

1. A friend has asked you to explain what holiness as love looks like. Take the time to write out your answer. Be sure to include key concepts such as who God is, what He desires for us, and what our response should be.

2. What were some ideas in this chapter that you most struggled with? Why? Who can you go to for assistance in thinking through these issues?

3. All of us run the risk that our love will be trumped by legalism. How can we ensure that our love for God will always supersede the rules we follow?

Emotions to Process

1. A kindergarten teacher was observing her classroom of children while they drew. She would occasionally walk around to see each child's artwork. As she got to one little girl who was working diligently, she asked what the drawing was. The girl replied, "I'm drawing God."

   The teacher paused and said, "But no one knows what God looks like."

   Without missing a beat, or looking up from her drawing, the girl replied, "They will in a minute."

   If you're really living a close relationship with God, then the people around you could draw their picture of God and it might look surprisingly like you. How does this make you feel? Why?

2. Our understanding of and ability to love is often based on how we have been loved. Take some time to reflect on how you have been loved by others. Do you see any problems that could make it difficult for you to accept God's love fully? If so, what are they, and how will you address them?

3. Pick one of the stories from this chapter (or from other parts of the book) and share how it impacted you.

Actions to Practice

1. The first ("Love the Lord your God") and second ("Love your neighbor as yourself") greatest commandments are easy to talk about but much harder to live. Take a few moments and create a list of the ways you feel God calling you to honor these two commandments. Carry it around with you this week and place a checkmark next to each of the things you actually do.

2. John Wesley taught the following prayer to his followers. Pray it each morning and evening in the next few weeks, and allow its simple words to instill in you a desire to be perfect in Christ.

   > Almighty God, all hearts stand wide open before You, every single person's desires are known by You, and there is not a secret in the world that You do not already know.
   > Wash clean all of our heart motives
   > Through the work of Your Holy Spirit
   > So that we may love You as we were intended to
   > And in so doing, may we give You all of our praise
   > Through Jesus Christ our Lord, Amen.[28]

SECTION 3

FREEDOM FOR OTHERS

HOLINESS AS CHARACTER AND POWER

CHAPTER 5
CHASING LIONS
CHOOSING TO LOVE OTHERS FOR THE SAKE OF GOD

*"To show great love for God and our neighbor we need not
do great things. It is how much love we put in the doing
that makes our offering something beautiful for God."*
—*Mother Teresa of Calcutta,* A Gift for God

The Bible is full of interesting characters. A boy who kills a heavily armored giant with just a slingshot. A slave girl who becomes Queen and saves an entire nation from extinction. A king who has it all and throws it away for a one-night stand. A virgin girl who gives birth to the savior of the world. A radical Jew intent on wiping out this new movement called Christianity who, after his encounter with Jesus, joins the very movement he tried to extinguish and becomes the greatest missionary the church has ever known. And so on.

One of the more interesting characters I find in Scripture is Benaiah. His story is found in 2 Samuel 23:20. It's only one verse, but it is jampacked with action and intrigue: "Benaiah son of Jehoiada was a valiant fighter from Kabzeel, who performed great exploits. He struck down two of Moab's best men. He also went down into a pit on a snowy day and killed a lion."

It's not every day that you read about someone killing a lion. My guess is that the closest you've ever been to a lion was seeing one at the zoo or circus. I've had the opportunity to see one up close and personal—its huge mane wrapped around its head making it seem twice as big as it was, the taut muscles ready to spring, the ferocious teeth bared, and the paws with their terrible claws ready to swipe. I was scared! Fortunately, there was a six-inch thick pane of glass between the two of us!

Not so with Benaiah. According to this verse, Benaiah faced this lion one-on-one in the ultimate example of bravery and courage. It would have been impressive enough had Benaiah slew the lion out on the plains in the middle of summer, when the ground would have been dry, the footing sure, and the sky clear. But that's not what happened. Instead, this lion was in a pit which severely limited movement, and the snow made the ground messy and wet. But as amazing as even that was, there is one other qualifier here that we need to take into account. Benaiah wasn't the first one in the pit. The lion was. Benaiah *chose* to go in the pit in order to kill the lion!

I guess the reason I'm so intrigued by Benaiah is that he chose to go into the pit after the lion. It would have been so easy for him to walk on by, knowing that the lion was in the pit, and, therefore, not a threat to his safety. However, self-centeredness was not a part of Benaiah's character. He wasn't just concerned with his safety but also with the safety of those around him. Rather than assuming that someone else would come along to deal with the lion, or that the lion would just die and the problem would take care of itself, Benaiah chose to go in after the lion.

Benaiah is a real-life hero because he was willing to give all he had in order to help others. This is one of the defining characteristics of holiness—a spirit of selflessness that acts for the good of others without undue concern for credit. It is the impulse to do good simply because it is the thing to do and it is what the kingdom of God is all about.

In this chapter, we will explore together a very simple and yet profoundly rich idea: *holiness should always result in a life lived for others.* Toward that end, we will examine how holiness results in a life of service by studying two passages of Scripture, one from the Old Testament and one from the New Testament. As we do this, it is my hope that we will begin to understand what this life lived for others looks like.

LIVING FOR OTHERS IN THE OLD TESTAMENT

The Old Testament passage is found in Isaiah 58:1-12. (Go find your Bible and take a moment to read it.) This passage can be divided into two opposing sections—verses 1-5, which describe the current status of things, and 6-12, which prescribe the way things should be. In the first five verses, the author describes the religious people of his day. Notice all of the good things they are doing:

- Praying to God daily
- Eagerly desiring God
- Seeking Yahweh's will so their decisions will be just
- Wanting God to be near.

In short, these were the "holy" people of this time. And yet . . . God calls them out, claiming that they are in rebellion against Him. These religious people are consumed with self-interest. They are only concerned with their own world, needs, and desires.

Remember the historical context here. Jerusalem is in shambles; most everything (including the Temple) was destroyed a few years earlier. There are some who have learned to use the situation to their advantage. These people have managed to build nice homes and enjoy a good life, while all around them are others who are poor, destitute, and homeless.

It's not enough that they enjoy their prosperity while everyone around them is hurting. They then proceed to complain to God because He doesn't seem to be listening to them. They talk about it in terms of fasting. But to them, fasting had become a way of "pushing a button" to get God to act, or just a religious practice to appear holy.[29]

It's to this situation that God responds. He makes it plain that their fasting is a sham. Their religious actions have no impact on the rest of their lives. Their fasting is empty, devoid of life-changing impact. In contrast, God offers up a different view of fasting, the type of fasting that pleases Him most. This fasting would not only begin to redefine how people worshiped, it would also redirect their focus from inward to outward.

In verses 6-12, God puts forward three ways in which we can serve Him, and in so doing, serve those around us. You may want to go ahead and reread these verses. Realize this is challenging stuff, and may make you feel a bit uncomfortable. That's OK—I'm the one writing it and I'm not all that comfortable with the implications. Don't feel overwhelmed when you read this. Simply read it with an open heart and mind and give God permission to move in your life as He sees fit.

1. "To loose the chains of injustice and untie the cords of the yoke, to set the oppressed free and break every yoke" (v. 6). The religious people had used their position to take advantage of those around them. That in part explains why they keep getting richer while those around them stay mired in poverty. God reminds them that if they were to be truly holy people, it would require that they be holy in all of their relationships: personal, work, school, church, and community. No longer can they pretend that it's permissible to use others for their gain. No longer can they use their power to keep others down just so they can enjoy the finer things of life. And most importantly, no longer can they hold others in bondage

by slavery or servitude. In essence, Yahweh says, "You complain all the time about Jerusalem still being in bondage to Persia, wondering why I don't do something to liberate you. What a bunch of hypocrites, for you turn around and do the same exact thing to your fellow countrymen, putting them in chains."

Obviously we don't put people in chains today. Or do we? The chains may not be physical, but has there been someone that you've used to get your way? Perhaps it was a boy who you flirted with in order to make your boyfriend jealous. Maybe it was making another player look bad so you would win the starting spot on the basketball team. It might even be the person in your youth group about whom you spread rumors concerning their spiritual life just so you could have that last spot on the worship team. These are all forms of oppression and bondage.

2. "Is it not to share your food with the hungry and to provide the poor wanderer with shelter—when you see the naked, to clothe him . . ." (v. 7a). The word "share" in this passage is powerful. It literally means "to break in two." As I've thought about this, I've come to a somewhat startling realization. What God is demanding is this: if you've got food and see someone who's hungry, give half of your food to that person. If you see someone who is homeless, take him or her in, allowing them to live in your house. Look through your closet and give away clothes to those who need them. (Not just the yucky clothes you don't like or last year's fashions that you wouldn't be caught dead in. Instead, make sure the person is dressed as nice as you are!)

3. "and not to turn away from your own flesh and blood" (v. 7b). God isn't talking about physical blood relatives, but rather the fact that the people were refusing to acknowledge the need of their fellow Hebrew brothers and sisters. In other words, they conveniently turned a blind eye to the needs of those around them. However, Yahweh declares, it isn't enough just to meet the needs of their blood relatives, nor even to meet the needs of their fellow countrymen. Instead, equality should be like the air they breathe and mutual respect present, not only with other Israelites, but also with the resident alien: "When an alien lives with you in your land, do not mistreat him. The alien living with you must be treated as one of your native-born. Love him as yourself, for you were aliens in

Egypt. I am the LORD your God" (Leviticus 19:33-34). God makes it clear: In the same way that you were loved and cared for when you were most vulnerable, you need to learn to love in a way that graciously receives the stranger in your midst.

John Wesley, the father of the Wesleyan-Holiness movement and one of the most ardent supporters of holiness, would have loved this passage, for he understood that all of our money was given to us by God. It was not our money to do with as we pleased. It was God's and He was simply entrusting it to us to do His work. Therefore, Wesley defined wealth as anything beyond the bare necessities of survival—food, clothing, and shelter. Everything else, according to Wesley, was for the care of those who needed it most. Think about that—after you pay your rent, buy food, and pay for enough clothes to get by, everything else you earned would be for those in need. In fact, Wesley so strongly believed in the idea that God had entrusted His financial resources into our care that he believed that if we used those resources for ourselves instead of others, we were robbing God. For Wesley, it was an act of worship, for if we were worshiping only God, then our use of God's resources would always be for others.

One of the primary concepts this passage teaches us is this: Holiness can't be relegated to just the religious areas of our life—church, youth group, mission trip, fall retreat, and so on. If it doesn't impact our whole life—every single area—then it's not really holiness.

LIVING FOR OTHERS IN THE NEW TESTAMENT

The New Testament passage is found in Luke 10:25-37. Take a moment to read it. When Jesus was asked by an expert in the law what the greatest commandments were, He turned the tables by asking the question of the so-called expert. The man answered, "'Love the Lord your God with all your heart and with all your soul and with all your strength and with all your mind'; and, 'Love your neighbor as yourself'" (v. 27). Perhaps no scripture is more central or significant for the church's understanding and practice of the ideal of Christian perfection than this verse.

This is a very familiar passage but I wonder if we've ever really understood the whole story. Most of us, I would guess, don't have the background knowledge that this expert in the law had. In summing up these two commandments, the expert in the law draws from two Old Testament passages with which he would have been very familiar due to his studies.

The first passage is drawn from the first part of the *Shema*, a central verse in Jewish life and belief. It is found in Deuteronomy 6:4-9, "Hear, O Israel: The LORD our God, the LORD is one. Love the LORD your God with all your heart and with all your soul and with all your strength."

Originally, the Shema was just the first verse, and was later expanded to include the following verses about keeping God's commandments in the front of your mind and passing them on to your children. But it is this first verse which was most important, for it was an affirmation and a declaration of Judaism's faith in one God. Therefore, in reciting this verse, the expert in the law makes it clear that the first priority is to love God. If we fail to do this, nothing else really matters.

However, it's the passage from which the second commandment is drawn, found in Leviticus 19:11-18, which I found particularly intriguing:

> Do not steal. Do not deceive or cheat one another. Do not bring shame on the name of your God by using it to swear falsely. I am the LORD. Do not defraud or rob your neighbor. Do not make your hired workers wait until the next day to receive their pay. Do not insult the deaf or cause the blind to stumble. You must fear your God; I am the LORD. Do not twist justice in legal matters by favoring the poor or being partial to the rich and powerful. Always judge people fairly. Do not spread slanderous gossip among your people. Do not stand idly by when your neighbor's life is threatened. I am the LORD. Do not nurse hatred in your heart for any of your relatives. Confront people directly so you will not be held guilty for their sin. Do not seek revenge or bear a grudge against a fellow Israelite, but love your neighbor as yourself. I am the LORD (NLT).

The command of God in these verses is simple justice for your neighbor and compassion for the vulnerable.

This sounds easy enough, but when we attempt to practice it, we quickly realize that it requires a lot more of us than we imagined. What does it really mean to practice justice? What does it really mean to live compassionately? Let's explore each of these in turn.

PRACTICING JUSTICE

One way we can define justice, and the Bible seems to support this understanding, is that justice is about recognizing that all people have things which belong to them and making sure they get to keep those things. This also means that if someone else has taken those things, then part of justice is helping people get their possessions back. The problem, of course, is that once we have possessions which aren't ours to begin with, we soon become accustomed to using and enjoying those possessions, to the point that we find them incredibly hard to give up. In fact, we get annoyed when we think someone wants to take away what is "ours." Perhaps a story I heard recently will help illustrate this point.

A woman at the airport was waiting for her flight to board. Feeling a bit hungry, she went to one of the convenience stores, purchased a pack of Oreos, and put them in her carry-on bag. When she arrived at her gate, she ended up sitting next to a guy who wore old, tattered clothes. She didn't want to sit there, but it was the only seat available.

After a few minutes, her hunger pains worsened, so she proceeded to open the pack of Oreos that were lying on the armrest and took a cookie. A few seconds later, the man sitting next to her also took a cookie. She was shocked! After a few minutes, she took another one, watching covertly out of the corner of her eye, and sure enough, a minute later, the gentleman took another cookie. *How dare he eat my cookies!* she thought. There was just one cookie left, but before she could move to get it, the man picked it up. The woman glared at him, but the man proceeded to break the cookie in half and give her one-half. Well, at this, her blood pressure started rising as her rage began to build. *Now he's mocking me,* she thought, *acting as if he is being generous when they're really my cookies.* She was going to scold him good for taking her cookies.

Just then the announcement came that his flight was now boarding. The man got up, graciously smiled at the woman, and left. The woman really was hot. Not only did that guy eat her cookies, but she didn't even have the satisfaction of chewing him out for doing so! So she sat there and fumed. A few minutes later, her flight was announced. She reached into her bag to retrieve her boarding pass and was shocked—for in her bag was the pack of Oreos she had bought at the store.[30]

This woman is not unlike us, for sometimes we possess things that really don't belong to us for so long that we begin to think they are ours. And like that woman, when we finally do notice that what we have is not ours but someone else's, it is often too late, and we end up with nothing more than regret.

Justice is not just something we do, it becomes who we are, as it emerges out of a life of holiness. Scripture links our love of God and love of neighbor: "If anyone boasts, 'I love God,' and goes right on hating his brother or sister, thinking nothing of it, he is a liar. If he won't love the person he can see, how can he love the God he can't see? The command we have from Christ is blunt: Loving God includes loving people. You've got to love both" (1 John 4:20-21, TM). We can't live one kind of love without the other. They go together.

We are called to do justice in the same way that God does justice. So how do we *do* justice in this world? How do we live lives that seek to restore things to their rightful order? In order to do justice, we first have to understand the world of those we seek to help. This is where the other command, compassion for the vulnerable, can help us.

LIVING COMPASSIONATELY

Henri Nouwen and some friends wrote a wonderful book titled *Compassion.* In the book, he describes compassion in this way:

> The word *compassion* is derived from the Latin words *pati* and *cum*, which together mean "to suffer with." Compassion asks us to go where it hurts, enter into places of pain, to share in brokenness, fear, confusion, and anguish. Compassion challenges us to cry out with those in misery, to mourn with those who are lonely, to weep with those in tears. Compassion requires us to be weak with the weak, vulnerable with the vulnerable, and powerless with the powerless. Compassion means full immersion in the condition of being human.[31]

"Full immersion in the condition of being human." That may seem like a weird phrase, but what Nouwen is basically saying is this: we can only really experience with others their pain, loneliness, joy, and surprise *if we are with them*. There is no other way. We can't practice compassion from a distance. It isn't enough just to send our monthly check to sponsor a child halfway around the world or to listen to a missionary share about her experiences and silently thank God it's her and not you. No, the type of compassion that God calls us to practice comes from being present with those in need. This is an investment of more than just our money or time. It is an issue of presence, an investment of our very lives.

Thankfully, we don't do this alone, for "when we are one with those in need, we must realize that Jesus is already there in our midst. Wherever there are poor in the world, wherever there are people in need, Jesus is already among them. We do not bring Jesus with us."[32]

THE GOOD SAMARITAN

Let's go back to our New Testament example of living for others. Not quite satisfied with Jesus' answer that this was enough, the expert in the law pushes back: "Just who is my neighbor?" The expected reply would be something like, "Your relative and your friend." Then the expert would be able to say that he has done that much and thereby enjoy honor among the people listening. However, Jesus proceeds to teach him the answer to this question by telling the parable of the Good Samaritan (Luke 10:29-37).

A man is robbed and left by the side of the road. Three people come by his position. The first, a priest, chooses to pass by on the other side. His actions would have been easy to justify from the perspective of the audience listening to Jesus. To risk approaching him could mean ceremonial defilement, especially if the person were actually dead. The second person to come by was a Levite—someone who assisted the priests in the Temple. The Levite also sees the wounded man and passes by. Again, the audience would have thought this was permissible. After all, the road is dangerous, and if the Levite stops to help he could become the next victim of violence.

Finally, a third man, a Samaritan, passes by. The Samaritans were a mixed race—hated by the Jews because they thought the Samaritans had watered down the Jewish religion. Yet in the story, the Samaritan chooses possible defilement in assisting the man. He runs the risk of being attacked by robbers. Despite all of the risks, the Samaritan is the one who chooses to help the wounded man.

The audience who heard this passage would have been flabbergasted that the Samaritan, not the priest or the Levite, was the hero of the story. Jesus then proceeds to ask those assembled, "Which of these three do you think was a neighbor to the man who fell into the hands of robbers?" (v. 36). The expert in the law, the one who had been trying to justify his actions, humbly realizes the error of his ways and gives the only response possible: "The one who had mercy on him" (v. 37a). And Jesus gives a simple command: "Go and do likewise" (v. 37b).

CHRISTLIKE COMPASSION

So what do these two passages on serving others have to do with holiness? Everything! As we learn to love God with all our heart, soul, mind, and strength, God's love begins to fill us up. However, I would suggest that it does not become "perfect" love until it is brimming over the top, finding its way into the lives of others as we share life together. I think Mother Teresa understood this concept when she wrote:

> I know that when I touch the limbs of a leper who stinks I am touching the body of Christ the same as when I receive the Sacrament. This conviction of touching Christ under the appearance of a leper gives me a courage which I would not have otherwise. Today once more, Jesus comes among His own, and His own do not know Him. He comes in the very hurt bodies of our poor. Jesus comes to you and me, and often, very often, we let Him pass without noticing.[33]

Mother Teresa discovered the secret that we who follow Jesus always receive more than we give, for we find our reward in the joy of the people whom we serve.

The closer we are to Jesus, the more Christlike we become, the more we begin to see the world as Jesus sees it. And because we are becoming more like Jesus in our pursuit of holiness, we will want to do the things Jesus does. Becoming holy calls us, with Jesus, to be personally present among the poor, the disenfranchised, and those on the margins of society.

Henri Nouwen writes, "Here we see what compassion means. It is not a bending toward the underprivileged from a privileged position. It is not a reaching out from on high to those who are less fortunate below. It is not a gesture of sympathy for those who fail to make it in the upward pull. On the contrary, compassion means going directly to those people and places where suffering is most acute and building a home there."[34]

May we all learn to let the love of God flow naturally to the world around us as we seek to be holy people—not so we will feel better about ourselves, but so that we may be a reflection of who Jesus is in us.

YEAH, RIGHT . . .

I have a hunch that some of you have read this chapter and are thinking to yourself, "Yeah, right. As if I could do those types of things." It probably doesn't seem realistic that we could love those who have hurt us, live in compassion with those who are different from us, and do justice for those we don't like. Yet, that's exactly what God calls us to do.

During World War II, the Nazis occupied Yugoslavia. Civil war broke out, and Serb fought Serb. In addition, hundreds of thousands of Orthodox Christians were tortured or massacred by the Croatians under the direction of the Nazis. Hosts of other Serbs were sent to Nazi death camps.

A Serbian Orthodox Bishop, Nikolai Velimirovic, chose to speak out against Naziism. He was arrested and sent to the infamous Dachau concentration camp, where he suffered horribly. While in the camp, he realized that he had one of two choices: (1) he could harbor bitterness in his heart against those who had done this terrible injustice, or (2) he could seek to love them like God wanted.

Needless to say, to choose the latter option was far from easy. After all, these were the people who were killing millions of Jews. Atrocities were committed daily by those who imprisoned him. And Bishop Nikolai himself experienced mental and physical torture. Yet somehow, with God's help, Bishop Nikolai was able to learn to love his enemies.[35] He even wrote a prayer asking God to bless his enemies and not curse them. In the prayer he tells God that he personally blesses them and refuses to curse them.[36]

The first time I read Bishop Nikolai's prayer, I thought to myself, "Now that was a man of God." I mean, he prayed for his enemies. I've been known to pray about my enemies, but it was more a prayer asking God to deal with them! Bishop Nikolai prayed *for* his enemies.

A CHANGE IN PRAYER

The key in living this type of life is prayer. I'm not talking about a prayer here and there for others. No, our prayers for others, including our enemies, must be a regular and consistent part of who we are as holy people. "To pray for others means to make them part of ourselves. To pray for others means to allow their pains and sufferings, their anxieties and loneliness, their confusion and fears to resound in our innermost selves. To pray, therefore, is to become those for whom we pray."[37] When we pray, we discover our neighbor's real worth. And when we pray for others in this way, "we meet Christ, and in him all human suffering. In service, we meet people, and in them the suffering Christ."[38]

If Christlikeness is our goal, then there could be no higher compliment we could receive than for someone to say that they see Jesus in us. When we engage in ongoing service to those around us, loving them in the same way that Christ loves us, then we *are* being Jesus. This is one of the defining characteristics of holiness.

Questions to Ponder

1. Benaiah *chose* to go after the lion, even though he knew it was a

risky proposition. What types of risks might God be calling you to take that would stretch you beyond your comfort level?

2. This chapter suggests some "hard sayings" about what God calls us to do as part of our quest for holiness. Take a moment to reexamine the requirements listed in Isaiah 58. How difficult will it be for you to accept these practices in your life? What changes will you need to make to live this way?

Feelings to Process

1. When you consider the command to "love your neighbor as yourself" (Matthew 22:29), how does this make you feel? Do you experience it as a burden—something you have to do and if not it produces guilt? Or do you see it as the natural overflow of your love relationship with Jesus Christ? Does it make any difference which view we take in our attempts to be holy people?

2. The life of service God calls us to is at best uncomfortable; at worst, it completely upsets everything we thought was important. As you think about your hopes and dreams for the future, look deep inside and ask yourself how open you are to following God's plan, even if it means the loss of those hopes and dreams.

Actions to Practice

1. Mother Teresa is perhaps the greatest modern-day example of someone who willingly gave her life to God for the sake of others. Following are some of her quotes which reflect her understanding of what our role is as God's ambassadors to the world around us. Select one or more of these quotes, write it on an index card, and carry it with you all week as a constant reminder of what God is calling you to do.

- "We can do no great things, only small things with great love."
- "Every time you smile at someone, it is an action of love, a gift to that person, a beautiful thing."
- "I am a little pencil in the hand of a writing God who is sending a love letter to the world."
- "There should be less talk; a preaching point is not a meeting point. What do you do then? Take a broom and clean someone's house. That says enough."
- "Let us more and more insist on raising funds of love, of kind-

ness, of understanding, of peace. Money will come if we seek first the kingdom of God—the rest will be given."[39]

2. Augustine wrote a beautiful prayer which summarizes this chapter well. I've contemporized it here. Read it through slowly, asking yourself what needs to happen for this prayer to become yours:

"O Lord, You who were rich beyond belief yet chose for our sakes to become poor, and who promised in the Scriptures that whatever we do for the least of our brothers and sisters, You will accept as if we had done it to You. Give us peace, we humbly pray, to be always willing and ready to minister to others, as You give us the strength and opportunity, and in so doing to extend the blessings of Your Kingdom all over the world; we do this to Your praise and glory, for You who are God above all, worthy of all blessing both now and forevermore."[40]

CHAPTER 6

LIONS AND LAMBS
THE COMMUNITIES THAT SHAPE OUR CHARACTER

*I came to know about God through my early initiation;
I came to know God through a life of Christian practices,
embodied in community."—Daryl Tippens*, Pilgrim Heart

When I was in high school and would go out with my friends or on a date, my mother would always wish me well, give me a kiss on the cheek, then look me in the eye and simply say, "Don't forget, Jim, you are a Hampton."

Of course, my mom wasn't worried that I would forget my name or my street address. Rather, she was concerned that, alone with my girlfriend, while attending a party after the football game, or while hanging out with some friends, I might forget who I really was. In other words, she was worried that I might forget the values that she and my father had instilled in me, and in so doing, participate in an activity which did not fit our family's characteristics and morals. She was concerned that I might lose my identity.

"Don't forget you are a Hampton," were her parting words to me each time I left home. And truth be told, they were words that I needed to hear because those words reminded me of who I really was.

All of us are called to live in the identity with which we were created. The problem, of course, is that there are a multitude of voices calling out to us, all with a different understanding of who we should be. While some of those voices may be helpful, most are not. In fact, I would suggest that most of those voices calling out to us are offering a false identity, an identity that runs counter to what Christ calls us to have.

GOD IMPARTS IDENTITY

Before you and I were even born, God desired that we would come to not only love Him, but imitate Him in our lives. God's hope was that you and I would find our very purpose for being in Him, and in so doing, find our identity. But before we can begin to live in that identity, we must first understand that our identity is based on who God is. Therefore, it's important that we begin by looking at God's character.

We've already discovered in this book that *God is love* (1 John 4:8) and that more than anything, He desires to have an intimate love relationship with each of us. We see this beautifully illustrated in the third chapter of Matthew. Jesus has come to John the Baptist to be baptized in the Jordan River. Although John initially protests, he does what he needs to do and baptizes Jesus. As Jesus comes up out of the water, Scripture tells us that "At that moment heaven was opened, and he saw the Spirit of God descending like a dove and lighting on him. And a voice from heaven said, 'This is my Son, whom I love; with him I am well pleased'" (Matthew 3:16-17).

Jesus heard the voice when He came out of the Jordan River, which reminded Him just how much God loved Him. You and I need to hear that voice, too. It is a very important voice that says, "You are My beloved son; you are My beloved daughter. I love you with an everlasting love. I have molded you together in the depths of the earth. I have knitted you in your mother's womb. I've written your name in the palm of My hand and I hold you safe in the shade of My embrace. I hold you. You belong to Me and I belong to you. You are safe where I am. Don't be afraid. Trust that you are Mine, My beloved. For that is who you truly are. That is your identity." God's amazing love for us is at the core of who God is.

The prophet Isaiah gives us another description of who God is, describing Him in this way:

But now, this is what the LORD says—he who created you, O Jacob, he who formed you, O Israel: "Fear not, for I have redeemed you; I have summoned you by name; you are mine. When you pass through the waters, I will be with you; and when you pass through the rivers, they will not sweep over you. When you walk through the fire, you will not be burned; the flames will not set you ablaze. For I am the LORD, your God, the Holy One of Israel, your Savior (43:1-3*a*).

THE PURPOSE OF RULES

According to Scripture, our **God is a holy God**, who not only makes it possible to pattern our lives after His, but expects us to do so. While this understanding of God is found throughout Scripture, perhaps nowhere is it more evident than in Leviticus 20. If you're like me when I was a teenager, you probably avoid reading Leviticus because it seems to be just chock-full of "Thou shall nots." But to really understand why there were so many rules to follow and things to avoid, you have to understand the culture in which Israel found herself. That's easy—look around. Israel was surrounded by a culture not unlike our own. They were surrounded by people who worshiped false gods and who indulged their every desire. Think the worst of "spring break wild behavior" and throw in some little god statues and some incense.

Once you have that picture in your mind, it becomes easier to see what God was doing. God never intended for the laws and commandments He gave to be constrictive. In fact, when God gave rules (like He did to Israel in Leviticus 20), it was for their safety and protection. God knew that once Israel began living among other nations and tribes, the temptation to engage in the same sinful things these other countries were doing would be strong. God sought to keep them as His holy people; the rules, in essence, served as a boundary of protection around them.

These were not arbitrary rules God gave them. Rather, the rules He asked them to follow emphasized who God was and what He expected of Israel. All of the rules we find, for example, in books like Leviticus and Deuteronomy were meant to protect Israel, to keep her from falling prey to the temptations around her. The rules were seen by God not as a form of punishment but as an extension of His very character, because they were given out of His love for Israel.

Now that we know what God is like, we have a better sense of what we should be like. We know what our identity is—that of being a child of God, made in His image, and called to pattern our lives after Him. Our identity is based on our pursuit of God's holiness. But we all understand that knowing how we should be and actually living that way isn't always an easy thing to do. There are a lot of voices in the world around us that are offering conflicting claims about who we are to be, voices that try to shape our identity in ways that don't reflect our God. And it is sometimes difficult amid all of these conflicting claims to remember who we are supposed to be, to remember our true identity. God understood that it would be nearly impossible for us to do this all by ourselves. Simply put, very few of us would have the discipline necessary to always engage in those Christian practices which can help us be holy.

LIFE IN THE BODY

Throughout Scripture, we find the biblical writers repeatedly encouraging Christians to be the Body of Christ, to discover the value of living in community with one another. One such passage is found in Philippians. In this letter to the people of Philippi (see especially 1:27—2:4), Paul writes because he has heard reports that the church is being fractured, not by beliefs about important God issues but by personal differences. Paul knows that this church faces enough struggles from the outside without having to endure those from within their fellowship. So he writes to them this letter, appealing to them on the basis of his love for them (which stems from God's love for Paul).

This then is what Paul is calling the Philippians to. He reminds them that they have a dual citizenship, one on earth and one in the heavenly Jerusalem, and they should live lives that are worthy of both. Central to this is the idea that they are to live their lives in harmony with each other. Why did Paul choose to bring up this idea of harmony?

I think at the very outset, Paul wanted to remind the Philippians of the fundamental thesis that Christian sanctification cannot be reduced to an individualistic exercise. The struggles of the Christian citizen must be faced within the fellowship of the believing community, for it is there that we discover what it means to be holy people.

COMMUNITY OR INDIVIDUAL GROWTH?

Now I know that for some of you reading this, red flags are popping up all over the place. "Surely you're not saying that individuals cannot be holy?" No, of course not. But what I am saying, and what I believe Paul to be saying, is that we as individuals do not mature; rather the community of which we are a part matures, and we then are drawn into the growth of the community. Paul understood that without life in community, we cannot sustain or deepen Christian faith and life. In the book of Philippians great emphasis is placed upon the corporate nature of the Christian community. You see, Paul realized that the gift of the Spirit is not an individualistic gift which is received in isolation from the community. Rather, it is a personal gift that creates an organic creation with other Spirit-filled persons. If you have ever played any type of team sport you understand this principle. No matter how gifted one individual may be, he or she will never achieve the one goal of a championship without the assistance of his or her teammates.

I think that the process of sanctification is much like this. The equipment for maturity is only available within the community. The graces for spiritual maturing are distributed throughout the community in the form of complementary gifts. Each member has an essential gift which is his or her privilege to exercise within that community. In order for us to mature into the people Christ has called us to be, it is essential that we learn to function as a community.

I know this is a difficult concept to grasp, so let me see if I can help you better understand it through an illustration. When I was 16, I was at our local county fair. I raised sheep, and we would take them to the fair to compete for prizes and to sell them.

On one particular day, the main event of the afternoon was a horse-pulling contest. Various horses competed against one another to see how much they could pull. A harness was attached to each horse, which led to a large sled that would be covered with various weights. The smaller horses (weighing around 500 pounds each) went first, attempting to pull the sled about 15 feet, over the finish line. These horses could pull as much as 2,500 pounds. Then, the big horses (weighing between 1,000-1,500 pounds) came in. The eventual first place horse moved a sled weighing 4,500 pounds! Can you imagine? That would be the equivalent of a 150 pound man pulling a sled weighing 600 pounds! The runner-up horse pulled a little over 4,000 pounds.

Just before the event concluded, the owners of the first and second-place horses began talking, and they wondered how much the animals could pull if they worked together. They hitched both of them up and loaded the sled. To the surprise of everyone who was there, the two horses collectively pulled over 12,000 pounds! When they worked together, compensating for the areas where one might be weak, adjusting for the areas where the other was stronger, they were able to accomplish so much more than each could do individually.

As we who are part of the Christian community lean upon one another and seek to help one another on to maturity, we will not only grow but, like the two horses, we will be able to accomplish so much more for the kingdom of God than would be possible if we were all working alone. As Maria Harris, one of my favorite authors, has noted, "we are only fully persons when we are in community and in communion with one another."[41]

But there are some things which we as believers need to do. First of all, Paul makes it clear that we must be like-minded, having the same love and being one in spirit and purpose. This does not mean that Paul is insisting on everyone holding the same opinion, or that everyone must act exactly the same. I mean, after all, what would life be like if everyone was simply a clone of one another? If everyone in our faith community was the same, how could we possibly help each other in our areas of weakness? After all, we would all have the same weakness. And it would be pointless to offer our strengths to another in our community because they would have the same strengths.

LOVE YOUR NEIGHBOR

Watchman Nee was a Chinese evangelist. He once told a story about another Christian he knew in China. The man was a poor rice farmer, and his fields lay high on a mountain. Every day he pumped water into the paddies of new rice. And every evening he returned to find that an unbelieving neighbor who lived down the hill had opened the dikes surrounding the Christian's field to let the water fill his own. For a while the Christian ignored the injustice, but at last he became desperate. What should he do, he wondered? His own rice would die if this continued. How long could it go on?

The man went to his fellow Christians and explained the situation. These Christians prayed together and came up with a solution. The next day the Christian farmer rose early in the morning and first filled his neighbor's fields; then he attended to his own. Watchman Nee said that the neighbor of this man subsequently became a Christian, his unbelief overcome by a genuine demonstration of a Christian's love for others.[42]

Do you have that type of love for your neighbor? Even when those around you treat you wrongly, are you able to still practice love for them? Jesus thought this idea was important enough that He spoke about it:

You're familiar with the old written law, "Love your friend," and its unwritten companion, "Hate your enemy." I'm challenging that. I'm telling you to love your enemies. Let them bring out the best in you, not the worst. When someone gives you a hard time, respond with the energies of prayer, for then you are working out of your true selves, your God-created selves. This is what God does. He gives his best—the sun to warm and the rain to nourish—to everyone, regardless: the good and bad, the nice and nasty. If all you do is love the lovable, do you expect a bonus? Anybody can do that. If you simply say hello to those who greet you, do you expect a medal? Any run-of-the-mill sinner does that (Matthew 5:43-47, TM).

So Paul reminds us that the way we live out love for our neighbor is to consider others better than ourselves. The simplicity of Paul's language should not blind us to its difficulty. Those who really try to consider others better than themselves soon discover that this does not come naturally. It is too easy to introduce permissible exceptions to Paul's rule. We see someone who does something that doesn't fit *our* concept of holiness and we automatically assume that they are not a holy person.

However, no such exceptions are possible where true humility reigns. Instead we need to pay special attention to the things that concern and interest others. In order for the Holy Spirit to really move and work among us as a community of faith, it requires us to be open, honest, and vulnerable, learning to lean on one another. No longer can we be Lone Rangers who try to take care of all of our own problems without the help of others and then ride off merrily into the sunset. It is in Christian community that the persons that we least want to associate with and those least deserving have a rightful claim on all that we have and are.

Often the things that divide us have little to do with the essential purpose. They become more crucial to us than Christ and separate us from Him and divide us from one another. This is why Paul calls upon us to be one in spirit and purpose. We need to recognize that within that purpose there is room for many different methods and points of view. The true obstacle to unity, and consequently to holiness, is not the presence of legitimate differences of opinion but self-centeredness. It is only as we learn what it means to be humble, what it means to be like-minded, what it means to have the same love, and what it means to be one in spirit and purpose that we begin to function together as a community.

In California, there are giant redwoods which have stood tall against the howling storms for centuries now. You would think that with such an endurance record they would have deep roots that burrow into the mountainside and wrap themselves around huge boulders. Actually, however, they have shallow roots.

How can they survive so long? They grow in groves, and the roots of many trees intertwine. Thus they stand together against the many storms as if to announce to the north wind, "We stand together. If you are going to take one of us out, you will have to take us all." Sometimes a redwood does fall, almost always one that sprouted some distance from the others. Its roots could not reach those of the other trees. Even a giant redwood cannot stand when it has to stand alone.

Christians are like that too. We cannot stand alone; we really do need each other. This holy life is not a journey for solitary souls. The church is a called-out community, a group of sinners saved by grace who help each other on the way. You see, it is only within the life of holiness that we can find unity and harmony. And it is only as we live life as a community that we grow and mature into the likeness of God.

THE MARKS OF TRUE COMMUNITY

So the ultimate question becomes this: if we understand how important it is to live together in community as part of our pursuit of holiness, what should that community look like? For the answer to this, we look to Isaiah 11:1-10. Take a moment to read through this passage.

What would a community look like that somehow functioned like the vision Isaiah gives to us? Consider the imagery we are given: a community where the wolf and the lamb lie down together, where the lion and the oxen both live together without destruction. In this type of community, I believe there are three characteristics present which we need to practice.[43]

First, this kind of community is based on inclusiveness, rather than exclusiveness. It is a place where members aren't concerned with whether everyone looks and acts the same. And the members aren't concerned with who's in and who's out. In this community the focus is on accepting others as they are, rather than how we think they should be. Its members seek to help each person find a place where he or she can fit. The Christian community welcomes individuals who are different in their race, class, gender, status, power, and culture to become disciples of Jesus Christ.

Second, this community Isaiah describes is a safe place, where a person can come in and find warmth and acceptance, not hurt and rejection. Isaiah refers to this when he says that "The wolf will live with the lamb . . . the infant will play near the hole of the cobra, and the young child will put his hand into the viper's nest" (vv. 6, 8). Think what would happen if you were to put a wolf and a lamb in the same room. Whether that lamb survived for very long would depend entirely on how hungry that wolf was! Yet Isaiah states that in this community there will not be the typical conflict, destruction, or backstabbing that takes place in other communities. No longer will we worry about someone spreading rumors about us and causing damage to our good name. We will not have to worry about being overlooked for a position of leadership because it is more about popularity than qualifications. Instead, in this community, the ferocious appetites of lions and wolves, and their natural desire for lambs, is somehow tempered and changed. Their old way of doing things is gone, and a new way is in place.

Third, this community Isaiah describes is a place of healing and conversion. In this world, there are many lambs that come to the Church with an ear bit off or a leg that has been severed. All of us have those areas where we don't measure up according to the community standards, and we worry what others will think about us. Our backgrounds don't fit everyone else's, and we really seem to be on the outside looking in. Many of us bring to the table hurts that run deep and that have forever shaped our perception of ourselves. Yet, according to Isaiah, crippled lambs should be able to come to this kind of community and find a community that surrounds them, accepts them unconditionally as they are, and loves them back to health and wholeness.

In addition to healing, the Church should also be a converting community, for if lions are expected to lose the taste of blood from their mouths, it will take a major reorientation to living. In this community, lions will only learn to eat straw when they allow the Holy Spirit to transform them, changing not only their outward behavior but also their inward intentions. In our churches, both individually and collectively, we need to submit ourselves to the Spirit's work, allowing Him to change our intentions, realign our priorities, and adjust our attitudes so that we begin to see others the way Jesus sees them. Only then will we respond in the same way He did—with love, compassion, and justice.

A BETTER PLACE

The problem, of course, is that we live in a sin-filled world, a world where more often than not the wolf eats the lamb, the lion devours the oxen, and the child is bitten by the viper. This can be seen by the forces at work around us. We live in a world where power trumps powerlessness, where huge powerful nations attempt to dictate the course of all other nations. We live in a world where money drives what happens, and those without it have no opportunity. Even in the church, there are lions that roar, stalking their next prey, seeking to take yet another bite.

But oh, I wish that we lived in another kind of world. Can you imagine? There would be no such thing as bullies and those who are bullied. There would be no such thing as those who label others and assign them to groups to distinguish others from themselves. In this world, there would be no need to worry about how we fit in, for everyone would accept us as we are—warts and all. It would be a world where people choose to live in harmony with one another, seeking always the good of others. The people who chose to live this way would say crazy, absurd things, things like, "he who is least among you all—he is the greatest" (Luke 9:48); "If you want to enter in, you must become like a little child" (Matthew 18:3, author's paraphrase); and even, "If you want to find your life, you've got to lose it" (Matthew 10:39, author's paraphrase).

Think about how our homes, churches, denominations, and world would be different if we chose to live life this way. The reality is that the world around us will continue to operate according to principles of power, materialism, self-interest, fear, and survival of the fittest. We live in a world that is dominated by keeping and taking; there is really very little room for giving, and forgiving.

So the question comes down to this: How do we live out the type of vision Isaiah offers us? How do we live in such a way that we are more concerned with others than ourselves? How do we practice mutual concern and safety for one another? How do we practice in this community principles of inclusion, healing, and converting?

In short, there is nothing we can do in and of ourselves to make this kind of community possible. But it is possible because of God's work in our midst and His desire to create just this type of community. But once God makes it possible, it is up to us to follow His lead. It means that each person in that community chooses to submit himself or herself to God and allow Him to be sovereign in his or her life. It means that we individually and collectively seek to do the things Jesus would do rather than following our own or even the community's inclinations. It means that we allow God the sometimes painful process of removing those lion-like tendencies from our lives. Only then can we realize the type of community that both Paul and Isaiah describe. Only then can we experience growth in grace and maturation in holiness. Only then will we learn what it means to be more like Jesus as we see His life lived out among us.

Questions to Ponder

1. What keeps you from fully buying into this vision that Isaiah and Paul offer?
2. What would it take to make this vision come true?

Emotions to Process

1. In order for this type of community to become a reality, each of us needs to be willing to allow God the opportunity to remove those tendencies in our lives which keep this type of community from being a reality. When you think about allowing God to do this type of surgery, what is your gut feeling? Why do you feel this way?

2. In Kevin Graham Ford's book, *Jesus for a New Generation,* a young lady named Marisa speaks these words when talking about the church: "I mean, God's invisible, right? But when God lives in people, you actually see him, and feel him through his people. When Christians love and help you, it's like God himself is talking to you and touching you."[44] How do you feel about Marisa's comment? Does this describe the church you know? Why or why not?

Actions to Practice

1. Think about the difference it would make in our homes, churches, relationships, and local communities if we were committed to living the type of holy life described in this chapter. Consider just one way that you can begin to practice this in your life and commit to doing it.

2. Think about the lamb-like people around you. Choose one of those people and resolve to help them overcome their fear or mistrust of others by demonstrating what Christ would do if He were physically present.

EVERYDAY SAINTS
LIVING AS HOLY PEOPLE

"I have found the paradox, that if you love until it hurts, there can be no more hurt, only more love."—Mother Teresa of Calcutta, A Gift for God

The 11th chapter of Hebrews is a "Who's Who" of saints in the church. Such luminaries as Enoch, Noah, Abraham, Sarah, Moses, and even Rahab the prostitute appear in this list of people of faith. The people listed in this chapter are truly the best of the best, the ones who walked closest with God. Whenever I look at this list, I have to admit to feeling just a little inadequate.

As you may have noticed in chapter five, Mother Teresa has long been one of my heroes of the faith. When she was alive, she embodied many of the characteristics of God: compassion, love, mercy, kindness. She had a deep and abiding relationship with Jesus Christ, evidenced by her willingness to step outside of her comfort zone in order to minister to those that no one else would. Ministering to lepers was not easy, but Mother Teresa and the other Sisters of Charity did so and did it with joy. In fact, she once said, "The miracle is not that we do this work, but that we are happy to do it."

Many people consider Mother Teresa a saint, and in fact, the process has already begun in the Catholic Church to officially grant her status as a saint. She may well join the ranks of "official" saints such as Francis of Assisi, Teresa of Avila, Augustine, and Catherine of Sienna.

WHAT MAKES A SAINT

In the Roman Catholic church, there are now over 10,000 such saints. Some saints are known worldwide—people such as Paul, Patrick, Bernard of Clairveaux, and Joan of Arc. Others are less well known worldwide but are important to a specific region. What distinguished these people as saints is that they were recognized as being exceedingly close to God, and, after their death, had a miracle attributed to them.

For many Christians, saints are little more than legendary figures—"perfect Christians" with superhuman capabilities—who bear little relevance to their own daily struggles and concerns. We commonly assume that these were persons of near superhuman strength of purpose who, because of that strength, chose a life of uncommon spiritual hardship. They spent their lives in prayer and performing good works. Some of them were martyrs. Others founded religious orders. Others had visions or performed miracles. However, I've discovered that many of these saints were far from being pillars of strength before they had a radical connection with God. And even then, they were simply ordinary people whose hearts and imaginations had been captured by a vision and who, risking all, threw themselves entirely on the grace of God.

Over the last six months that I've been working on this book, I have come to think about holiness and sainthood somewhat differently than before, so I'd like to suggest another understanding of the word: *Saints are people who listen to God and try to do what He wants.* All of us who have experienced the holy love of God and are daily striving to love God and others in the same way we have been loved are saints. The New Testament word "saint" is actually the plural of the word we translate for "holy." In other words, according to the Bible, saints are holy people, and holy people are saints. You can't be one without being the other because they are flip sides of the same coin. Remember, holiness isn't what you do or don't do. It's who you are. It's the state of being a saint. When we understand that being holy is belonging to God, then we recognize that we are sacred people, saints who are different from the ordinary. We understand that holiness is about "belonging-to-God-ness,"[45] being His possession, so that we can love Him with all we have and love our neighbor as well.

In Romans 6:1-11, Paul reminds us that those who have identified with Christ have "died to sin" (v. 2), have been "baptized into Jesus Christ . . . into his death" (v. 3) and have been "raised from the dead through the glory of the Father . . . [to] live a new life" (v. 4). Our "old self was crucified with him" (v. 6), so that we are no longer under the control of sin. God, through the power of the Holy Spirit, has done all of this for us. Therefore, Paul, says, you must "count yourselves dead to sin but alive to God in Christ Jesus" (v. 11) *because in fact you actually are so.* On the basis of your union with Christ, Paul urges, *"become what you are."*[46] In other words, Paul is saying, "You've been bought with the blood of Jesus and made holy by the power of the Holy Spirit. You are a saint. Now live it!"

TWO REQUIREMENTS

There are only two requirements to being a saint. First a saint, a holy person, is learning to become so dependent on God that nothing else matters. As Cardinal Suhard once observed, to be a saint means "to live in such a way that one's life would not make sense if God did not exist."[47] Since the purpose of this book is to help you learn how to be holy, to have no other loyalties or allegiances, to "Love the Lord your God with all your heart and with all your soul and with all your mind and with all your strength" (Mark 10:30), one of the natural outcomes of that holy pursuit is that you will become a saint. And since holiness, as we've discovered, should impact every area of our lives every single day, we are called then to be everyday saints.

The second requirement to being a saint is that you learn to "love your neighbor as yourself" (Matthew 22:39). When we first became Christians, our prayers were largely self-centered. We asked for things like good health and success in life. But the more holy we become, the more our focus is on God, the more our prayers begin to change; we start praying for others, for a part of our sanctification is to make holy and set apart for God's use everything we touch. And when we do pray for ourselves, it is a prayer focused on this gift of perfect love. We ask God to enable us to love as He loves, to touch others as He did, to bring His Kingdom to earth here and now.

The world might say there are many reasons why God wouldn't want to use you or me, why we could never be an everyday saint. But consider the following people that God chose to use:

- Moses stuttered.
- David's armor didn't fit.
- Amos's only training was in the school of fig-tree pruning.
- Solomon was too rich.
- Abraham was too old.
- David was too young.
- Timothy had ulcers.
- Peter was afraid of death.
- Lazarus was dead.
- John was self-righteous.
- Naomi was a widow.
- Paul and Moses were murderers.
- Jonah ran from God.
- John Mark was rejected by Paul.
- Hosea's wife was a prostitute.

- Miriam was a gossip.
- Gideon and Thomas both doubted.
- Jeremiah was depressed and suicidal.
- Elijah was burned out.
- John the Baptist was a loudmouth.
- Martha was a worrywart.
- Mary was lazy.
- Samson had long hair.
- Noah got drunk.

While others might say that we're not worthy to be an everyday saint, Jesus says simply, "I've made them worthy."

Sure. There are lots of reasons why God shouldn't want us. But if we are utterly in love with Him, if we hunger for Him more than our next breath, He'll use us in spite of who we are, where we've been, or what we look like. That's what it means to be an everyday saint.

JUST THE BEGINNING

We who gather to worship God in the name of Jesus are never alone. There is a wider community of saints that unites believers across all boundaries of time and space. We can look for holiness, or saintliness, in the people of our ordinary lives, for saints exist today and are all around us. Their presence challenges us with the extraordinary possibilities of our ordinary existence. And they are both of the same material and a far cry from their stained-glass predecessors. Saints may never have started out as perfect people, but they are used by God to do His work.

As everyday saints, you and I are connected to something much bigger, deeper, and wider than our individual lives. We are a part of the story of God's salvation history. Millions who have come before us, millions spread all over the earth currently, and millions who will come after us are all a part of this grand and glorious story. We are part of the storyline which includes the great heroes and heroines of the faith—folk like Moses, Merriam, David, Esther, Mary, Paul, Catherine of Sienna, Teresa of Avila, Martin Luther, John Calvin, John Wesley, Billy Graham, Mother Teresa, and (insert your name).

GOD IN ALL

We have a tendency to divide our lives into compartments: family, school, friends, chores, church, part-time jobs, extracurricular activities, personal spiritual disciplines, our future, the past, and so forth. The problem is that too often in this pie chart of our lives, we relegate God's presence and work to one or two slices. For instance, we readily give God our

Sundays and possibly our Wednesday evenings. We offer Him our daily (?) devotions, tithes, and talents in service to the church and the world. In short, we only give God those pieces of the pie which are tied to "spiritual" stuff.

But God is present in so much more of our lives. When you're having a conversation with your friend while waiting for the school bus—God is there. As your taste buds explode when you savor the warm brownie melting in your mouth—God is there. When you are struggling with a homework assignment, wondering what in the world two trains going in opposite directions at different speeds has to do with real life—God is there.

The truth is that God is present in the everyday-ness of life. But there are a thousand voices calling out, vying for our attention, eager to be heard. And all of us have countless demands on our time, sapping our strength and focus, often leaving us too tired to even notice that God is present.

But part of what it means to be filled with the Spirit is the incredible awareness that God is present, vividly present, in every moment. When we allow God to fill us, we begin to see life for the first time the way God sees it. We recognize that every single thing we say, every thing we do, each action we undertake is an opportunity to participate in God's life.

When we recognize that holiness impacts all areas of our life, indeed all areas of our world as we live for God, then we will begin to see the saints that are all around us: saints immersed in the worlds of art, literature, music, business, education, politics, and in everyday life. We need saints to serve as prophets who challenge the church as well as the world to better reflect the justice and mercy of God. We need the witness of those saints, ancient and new, who have laid down their lives for their faith and for their neighbors. We need those saints who are able to see beyond the ordinariness of life to remind us of the ever-present God in our midst.

So we come to the end of this book. We've covered a lot of territory, and it hasn't been an easy journey. There were things we discussed which were filled with the promise and the hope of what can be when we learn to live in communities of holiness. We've examined some things that have been challenging as we recognize our own tendencies to have displaced loyalties. We've discovered some areas that have been downright painful as we learned how far we still have to go in the journey called holiness. Throughout our time together, my humble prayer has been that you would discover the incredible joy, peace, and aliveness that comes from living the holy life of an everyday saint. For indeed, you are one.

As we close, let me offer you this blessing:

May God bless you because you've chosen to do away with all other allegiances so that your focus is on Him and Him alone. May God bless you with discomfort at easy answers, half-truths, and superficial relationships so that you may live deep within your heart. May God bless you with anger at injustice, oppression, and exploitation of people, so that you may wish for justice, freedom, and peace. May God bless you with enough foolishness to believe that you can make a difference in this world, so that you can do what others claim cannot be done. And may God bless you with His holy love as you live out, for God and others, what it means to be a holy saint. Amen.[48]

Questions to Ponder

1. How would you have defined "saint" prior to reading this chapter? How has your understanding of the term changed?
2. What difference does it make when we learn to see God at work in the ordinary things of life?
3. As you reflect back on this book, what have been some of the most hopeful things you've read about your ability to live as an everyday saint? What particularly challenging issues make it seem more difficult to do so?

Feelings to Process

1. How hard is it for you to accept that you really are a holy saint of Jesus Christ? How does this make you feel?
2. Living a life of holiness can be both exhilarating and terrifying because we trust God implicitly to be in control of our lives. As you consider what it means to give God full control of your life, what do you see as the ramifications of such a decision? How would your life change as a result?
3. How will your life be different if you take the principles in this book seriously? Are you willing to do that?

Actions to Practice

1. Go back through each of the chapters and write down in one sentence what the central theme of each chapter is. This will give you a great summary of what it means to live as an everyday saint.

2. Educators understand that if something is really going to make a difference in our lives, we may need to hear it several times before it really sinks in and begins to create change. Think about how your own understanding of what it means to be holy has changed over the course of this book. Share with a trusted adult what you've learned from this study and commit with that person to continue to grow in holiness.
3. Now that you've had the opportunity to learn how to be a holy person, it's time to share that with someone else. Take the time to find a friend who needs to hear about this life-giving message and commit to finding a way to share it with them so they too can discover the joy of being an everyday saint.

GLOSSARY OF HOLINESS TERMS

In this book, some terms were used interchangeably to describe the work of God making us holy. Each of these terms has been used by Christians to describe either the process of becoming holy or to define the various aspects of holiness. This Glossary will attempt to briefly define each word to help you better understand it, and its role in the topic of holiness. You'll quickly notice that the definitions are often so close as to make them indistinguishable from one another.

Christian Perfection: God calls us to be holy as He is holy. Our ability to be holy people rests in the fact that we walk with God and we put our focus entirely on Him. Christian Perfection then is the combination of two important factors: (1) we who have been saved commit ourselves wholly to God, giving Him total control of our lives; and (2) God continually enables us, by the redirecting of our hearts and minds to Him, to become who we were created to be—people who love God with our whole heart, and reflect God's love to others. When we are able to do this, we then fulfill our purpose for being! This is not a perfection of *performance* (meaning all our behaviors are always right) but rather a perfection of *purpose* (our motives and intentions are pure and directed only to God). It is this latter understanding of perfection to which God calls us.

Entire Sanctification: This involves both a point in time when God cleanses our hearts from self-centeredness, and a continuing process whereby we become more like Christ over the course of our lives. When Christ, through the Holy Spirit, sets us free from the chains of our own selfish motives, and frees us to follow Him, then we also are empowered for service to others, as we seek to meet the needs of those around us. Entire sanctification most often occurs after our conversion (becoming believers in Jesus) and justification (what God does to make us right in His eyes), although some have been known to experience both so closely together as to make them indistinguishable.

Holiness: We know that God alone is holy, and that any other person or thing becomes holy only in relation to God. Holiness, then, is the work of God whereby He draws us to Him, purifying our motives and equipping us with His love so we can minister to the world around us. Through the process of holiness, we become everyday saints, those who depend solely on God for their life in order that they can truly love their neighbor in the same way God does.

Perfect Love: Love for God and for others is at the heart of this term. When we seek God with all of our hearts, and give God permission to move us from self-centeredness to God-centeredness, He then instills in us an agape love (a love which responds to things the way God would) for others. This "perfect love" is given to us by God always for the sake of changing the world around us for good.

Sanctification: The biblical word for sanctification is *hagiasmos* and means "to set apart for God," or "the setting apart for God." Sanctification has two parts to it. First, when God sanctifies (the verb form of sanctification) us, He sets us apart for himself. In doing so, God makes us holy because He is holy, ready to be used for His purposes. Second, an inner renewal takes place, whereby God, through the Holy Spirit, continues to make us pure so we can faithfully serve Him and minister to others.

SUGGESTED RESOURCES FOR FURTHER STUDY

Perhaps this book has developed in you a deep desire to learn more about this holy life of being an everyday saint. If so, here are some other books you might find particularly helpful in your passionate pursuit of God:

Cassell, Bo. *A Perfect Life: A Plain Account of Christian Perfection.* Kansas City: Barefoot Ministries, 2005.

Green, Tim. *Never Alone: Practicing the Presence of God.* Kansas City: Beacon Hill, 2005.

Hampton, Jim and Schoonover, Mike. *Vital Beliefs: Finding Our Place in the Story of God.* Kansas City: WordAction Publishing, 2001.

Harper, Steve. *The Way to Heaven: The Gospel According to John Wesley.* Nashville: Abingdon Press, 2003.

Nees, Tom. *Dirty Hands—Pure Hearts: Sermons and Conversations with Holiness Preachers.* Kansas City: Beacon Hill Press, 2006.

Nouwen, Henri J.M., McNeil, Donald P., and Morrison, Douglas A. *Compassion: A Reflection on the Christian Life.* New York: Image Books, 1982.

Oord, Thomas Jay and Lodahl, Michael. *Relational Holiness: Responding to the Call of Love.* Kansas City: Beacon Hill Press, 2005.

NOTES

1. Koontz, Dean. *One Door Away from Heaven*. Bantam, 2002, 596.

2. The Wesleyan tradition would be those churches that follow the teachings and basic theology of John Wesley. These would include many churches and organizations that would call themselves "holiness" groups, including Methodist, Church of the Nazarene, Wesleyan Church (obviously), Salvation Army, and others. John Wesley was a spiritual leader from the 1700s in England who came to the North American continent as a missionary and founded the Methodist denomination. They were called "Methodists" because they sought to practice holiness and they became known for their methods of incorporating spiritual holy habits into their lives.

3. Holiness is such a broad concept that the church has come up with several words to describe both the process of becoming holy, as well as particular aspects of what it means to be holy. While I recognize that words have specific meanings (especially to theologians, those whose career it is to talk about and study God), for the purpose of this book, I will use the following words interchangeably: holiness, sanctification, entire sanctification, Christian perfection, and perfect love. For a more nuanced understanding of each, please see the Glossary at the end of the book.

4. Hermiz, Tom. *Holiness: The Journey, The Joy, The Difference*. Kansas City: Beacon Hill Press of Kansas City, 2004, 21.

5. We often call this an act of consecration, whereby we give ourselves wholly to God and allow Him to use us as He sees fit. But as important as our role of consecration is in becoming holy, in the end we must recognize that holiness is entirely by grace. It is God who does it in us, not something we achieve by our own effort. We merely turn ourselves over to Him—that is what it means to consecrate ourselves.

6. In fact, according to Scripture, we begin the process of holiness the very moment we ask Jesus to forgive us and He takes residence in our lives. In theological terms, we call this justification or initial sanctification.

7. C. S. Lewis, "The Great Divorce," from *The Complete C. S. Lewis Signature Classics*, San Francisco: Harper San Francisco, 2002, 350-51.

8. Adapted from Eric Saperston in *Chicken Soup for the Teenage Soul,* Canfield, Jack, Hansen, Mark Victor, and Kirberger, Kimberly, eds. Deerfield Beach, FL: HCI Teens, 1997.

9. Adapted from Swindoll, Chuck. Dallas Seminary Daily Devotional E-mail, 2-7-05.

10. Maas, Robin. *Crucified Love: The Practice of Christian Perfection*. Nashville: Abingdon Press, 1989, 35.

11. Adapted from http://www.sermoncentral.com/sermon.asp?SermonID=91922, accessed 3/15/2007.

12. Mother Teresa as quoted in *Everything Starts from Prayer: Mother Teresa's Meditations on Spiritual Life for People of All Faiths*. Selected and arranged by Anthony Stern. White Cloud Press, 1998.

13. Otto, Rudolf. *The Idea of the Holy*. Oxford University Press, 1958.

14. This careful language reflects an important distinction—that we become like God, but we do not become "gods." We recognize that God make us holy, but it is a human holi-

ness—we are made righteous, but that doesn't mean we will never make mistakes, never forget anything, or never misjudge something because we don't know all the information. Only God himself is all knowing, we are not expected to know everything. This is a limitation of being human, and God understands this. (Even the pagan sun worshipers merely became suntanned, they didn't expect to turn into cosmic spheres of fire.)

15. Perfect. *Dictionary.com Unabridged (v 1.1)*. Random House, Inc. <http://dictionary.reference.com/browse/perfect>. Accessed January 29, 2007

16. Diaz, Gloria. "Quality Counts," Arizona Department of Economic Security, *The DEScriber* 9 (February 2002), p. 12

17. Kierkegaard, Søren. *Purity of Heart is to Will One Thing*. New York: Harper and Brothers, 1956), p. 72.

18. Greathouse, *Perfect Love*, p. 20.

19. Maas, p. 21.

20. Kendall, David. *Is Holiness Really Possible?* Kansas City: Beacon Hill Press, 2000, p. 35.

21. Maas, p. 30

22. However, this is no one-sided love. It is not the love of a person who develops a deep, abiding love for another, knowing all the time that this other person doesn't even know who they are. Rather this is the love of a God who not only knows us, but His capacity for loving us has no end. Again, consider the words of Robin Maas: "By the same token, the God whom we must learn to love to full capacity sets no limits to his love for us. The unlimited love of God promises to make saints out of the least promising material: us. Thus the doctrine of Christian perfection is as optimistic about God as the doctrine of original sin is pessimistic about human nature." Maas, p. 30.

23. Kendall, p. 48.

24. Wesley, John. *A Plain Account of Christian Perfection*. Beacon Hill Press, 1966. Note that this book has been updated into modern language in the title, *A Perfect Life*, by Barefoot Ministries®.

25. In choosing this position, I have been influenced both by Wesley and his many interpreters, particularly Mildred Wynkoop. This Nazarene theologian radically shaped my (and a whole generation of Nazarene pastor's) understanding of holiness as love rather than ethic, primarily through her book, *A Theology of Love*. Beacon Hill Books, 1972. Reading Wesley through this lens of love also seems to allow for this possibility: "It [Christian perfection] is a renewal of the heart in the whole image of God, the full likeness of Him that created it. In yet another, it is the *loving God with all of our heart, and our neighbor of ourselves . . . this is the whole and sole perfection . . ."* (*The Works of John Wesley,* ed. Thomas Jackson, 14 volumes. London: Wesleyan Conference Center, 1872; reprinted Grand Rapids: Baker Book House, 1978, 11:444, emphasis mine).

26. Benefiel, pp. 3-4.

27. Kendall, p. 49

28. Adapted from *John Wesley's Sunday Service of the Methodists in North America* (Nashville: The United Methodist Publishing House and the United Methodist Board of Higher Education and Ministry, 1984), p. 125.

29. One commentator helped illuminate this for me when he wrote that "in the Semitic way of speaking, 'fasting' meant more than refraining from eating. The word stood for all that

was implied in a self-righteous religiosity that divorced faith from love." Knight, George A. F. *The New Israel: Isaiah 56-66*, in *International Theological Commentary* (Grand Rapids: Eerdmans, 1985), p. 22.

30. An old story from several sources including http://www.snopes.com/crime/safety/cookies.asp, accessed 3/16/2007.

31. Nouwen, Henri J. M., McNeil, Donald P., and Morrison, Douglas A. *Compassion: A Reflection on the Christian Life.* New York: Image Books, 1982, p. 4.

32. Benefiel, Ron. "These Brothers and Sisters of Mine" in Nees, Tom (ed.). *Dirty Hands—Pure Hearts.* Kansas City: Beacon Hill Press, 2006, p. 27.

33. Mother Teresa. *A Gift for God: Prayers and Meditations.* New York: Harper and Row, 1975

34. Nouwen et al, p. 27.

35. Info taken from: <http://www.orthodoxinfo.com/general/stnikolai.aspx>.

36. Here is the prayer Bishop Nikolai wrote regarding his enemies and critics:

"Bless my enemies, O Lord. Even I bless them and do not curse them. Enemies have driven me into Your embrace more than friends have. Friends have bound me to earth; enemies have loosed me from earth and have demolished all my aspirations in the world.

"Enemies have made me a stranger in worldly realms and an extraneous inhabitant of the world.

"Just as a hunted animal finds safer shelter than an unhunted animal does, so have I, persecuted by enemies, found the safest sanctuary, having ensconced myself beneath Your tabernacle, where neither friends nor enemies can slay my soul.

"Bless my enemies, O Lord. Even I bless and do not curse them.

"They, rather than I, have confessed my sins before the world. They have punished me, whenever I have hesitated to punish myself. They have tormented me, whenever I have tried to flee torments. They have scolded me, whenever I have flattered myself. They have spat upon me, whenever I have filled myself with arrogance. Bless my enemies, O Lord. Even I bless them and do not curse them.

"Whenever I have made myself wise, they have called me foolish. Whenever I have made myself mighty, they have mocked me as though I were a [fly].

"Whenever I have wanted to lead people, they have shoved me into the background.

"Whenever I have rushed to enrich myself, they have prevented me with an iron hand.

"Whenever I thought that I would sleep peacefully, they have wakened me from sleep.

"Whenever I have tried to build a home for a long and tranquil life, they have demolished it and driven me out.

"Truly, enemies have cut me loose from the world and have stretched out my hands to the hem of your garment.

"Bless my enemies, O Lord. Even I bless them and do not curse them.

"Bless them and multiply them; multiply them and make them even more bitterly against me:

"So that my fleeing will have no return; So that all my hope in men may be scattered like cobwebs; So that absolute serenity may begin to reign in my soul; So that my heart may become the grave of my two evil twins: arrogance and anger;

"So that I might amass all my treasure in heaven; Ah, so that I may for once be freed from self-deception, which has entangled me in the dreadful web of illusory life.

"Enemies have taught me to know what hardly anyone knows, that a person has no enemies in the world except himself. One hates his enemies only when he fails to realize that they are not enemies, but cruel friends.

"It is truly difficult for me to say who has done me more good and who has done me more evil in the world: friends or enemies. Therefore bless, O Lord, both my friends and my enemies. A slave curses enemies, for he does not understand. But a son blesses them, for he understands.

"For a son knows that his enemies cannot touch his life. Therefore he freely steps among them and prays to God for them. Bless my enemies, O Lord. Even I bless them and do not curse them."

Source: Velimirovich, Bishop Nikolai. *Prayers by the Lake,* published by the Serbian Orthodox Metropolitanate of New Gracanica, 1999.

37. Nouwen et al, p. 115.

38. Nouwen et al, p. 117.

39. All of these quotes are taken from: Mother Teresa, *A Simple Path*, New York: Ballantine Books, 1995.

40. Taken from Castle, Tony. *The New Book of Christian Prayers*. New York: Crossroad, 1986, p. 265.

41. Harris, Maria. *Fashion Me a People: Curriculum in the Church*. Louisville: Westminister/John Knox, 1989.

42. Nee, Watchman. *The New Covenant*. Living Stream Ministry, 1999, p. 156.

43. I'm indebted to Dr. Steve Green for suggesting these categories in a sermon preached at Nazarene Theological Seminary on April 9, 1991.

44. Ford, Kevin Graham. *Jesus for a New Generation*. Downers Grove, IL: InterVarsity Press, 1995, p. 231.

45. A phrase suggested by Dr. Terrence Paige in a listserv discussion, December 8, 2006.

46. Greathouse, William. "A Pauline Theology of Sanctification" in Dunning, H. Ray and Wiseman, Neil B. (eds.), *Biblical Resources for Holiness Preaching*. Kansas City, Beacon Hill, 1990, p. 33.

47. As quoted in Ellsberg, Robert. "The Mystery of Holiness" in *Sojourners*, September-October, 1997. Accessed from: http://www.sojo.net/index.cfm/action/resources/index.cfm?action=magazine.article&issue=soj9709&article=970921 on January 24, 2007.

48. An adapted Franciscan blessing.